1988

SMOKING AMONG YOUNG ADULTS

Smoking Among Young Adults

M. MURRAY

Department of Psychology
University of Ulster

and

L. JARRETT
A. V. SWAN
R. RUMUN

Department of Community Medicine
United Medical and Dental Schools
of Guy's and St. Thomas' Hospitals
University of London

Avebury

Aldershot · Brookfield USA · Hong Kong · Singapore · Sydney

Published by

Avebury

Gower Publishing Company Limited
Gower House
Croft Road
Aldershot
Hants GU11 3HR
England

Gower Publishing Company
Old Post Road
Brookfield
Vermont 05036
USA.

British Library Cataloguing in Publication Data
Smoking among young adults.
  1. Cigarette habit——Great Britain
  2. Youth——Great Britain——Tobacco use
  I. Murray, M.
  306'.4   HV5745

ISBN   0 566 05467 1

Printed and bound in Great Britain by
Athanaeum Press Ltd, Newcastle upon Tyne

Contents

Contents

Acknowledgements

We would like to record our gratitude to the many individuals who have contributed to the creation of this book. In particular, we would like to thank the young adults who so willingly agreed to be interviewed and those who generously gave their time to complete and return the questionnaires. We would also like to thank the various members of the Department of Community Medicine, St. Thomas' Hospital Medical School, London for their constant support during the conduct of this study. We are particularly grateful to our secretaries both in St Thomas' and in the University of Ulster for their forebearance in typing and retyping the various versions of the text and to the computer services personnel for preparing and transferring the various computer files.

The Medical Research Council provided a project award to support this research. The original findings were submitted to that body in two reports entitled "MRC/Derbyshire Young Adults Study : Report on the First Stage" by M Murray and L Jarrett, and "MRC/Derbyshire Young Adults Study : Report on the Second Stage" by M Murray, L Jarrett, AV Swan and R Rumun. We are grateful to the Medical Research Council and to the Department of Health and Social Security for their continuing support for this research.

Some material from the first part of the study was previously reported by M Murray and L Jarrett in the Health Education Journal (1985) 44:18-26.

PART I
INTRODUCTION

1 Background to the study

1.1 Introduction

Smoking has been described as the single largest specific cause
of preventable disease and premature death in Western society.
According to the most recent report on the subject by the Royal
College of Physicians (1983) smoking accounts for 15 to 20% of
all deaths in Britain today. That report added that while it is
difficult to be precise at least 90% of the 70,000 deaths from
lung cancer, bronchitis and obstructive long disease and a
further 20% of the 180,000 deaths due to coronary heart disease
which occurred in Britain in 1981 are related to smoking. In
addition, those who smoke are more likely to suffer chronic ill-
health and as a consequence reduce their opportunity of living a
full active life.

In view of this compelling scientific evidence linking smoking
with subsequent ill-health why do so many people continue to
smoke and why do so many young people adopt smoking every year?
These questions have intrigued social and behavioural scientists
for decades.

The regular listings of publications by the Tobacco Advisory
Council and other bodies reporting the findings of research in
this area emphasise the vast amount of human effort which has
been expended in trying to solve this puzzle. However, a full
understanding of the phenomenon remains elusive. In a recent
review of some of the more recent research in this area McQueen
(1985) felt compelled to state that while 'much is known about
the attitudes of individuals towards smoking, and about how
people smoke (w)hat is less clear is why people smoke and why
they give up or start smoking'. He considered that one of the
reasons for this was that the focus of previous research has been
'on the knowledge, attitudes and practices of individual
smokers', while little attention has been given to 'the role of
society in perpetuating such individual behaviours'.

McQueen (1985) made three proposals for future research in
smoking behaviour: (1) monitoring and explaining long-term
trends in smoking; (2) multiple units of analysis based upon an
understanding of how data on behaviour collected at different

3

levels of observation can be combined; (3) elaboration of additional units of analysis. Under this third heading he claimed that "every decade brings new conceptual emphases. In the seventies the emphasis in behavioural research was on the relationships between attitudes and behaviour, and is well represented in the theory of reasoned action as propounded by Ajzen and Fishbein (1980). Emphasis in the current decade has shifted to a broad concern with the context of behaviour". Having been involved with research into smoking behaviour for the past decade we would broadly agree with McQueen's description of the inadequacies of previous research and with his proposals for future work in this area.

The research reported in this book is an attempt to consider the social psychology of smoking among young adults rather than provide further details of the attitudes and beliefs of the individual smoker or of the societal correlates of smoking. The project formed the final stage of a larger longitudinal study of the factors involved in the development of smoking among young people. That study began in 1974 and data collection on the smoking practices and associated characteristics of a large sample of young people continued for ten years. A series of journal articles and reports have detailed the basic findings of the earlier stages of the study (e.g., Banks, Bewley, Bland, Dean and Pollard, 1978; Bewley, Johnson and Banks 1979; Murray, Swan, Bewley and Johnson, 1983).

In 1981 it was decided to alter substantially the method and focus of the investigation. The earlier stages of the study had been survey based and concentrated on identifying which of the many social and psychological factors measured in the early stages of adolescence predicted later smoking. The final stage of the study, reported in the following chapters, put greater emphasis on the interview as a method of data collection, although these findings were supplemented by data collected in a large survey. The focus of this investigation was not on predictors of later smoking but on trying to explain smoking among young adults as a meaningful social practice.

The way an issue is defined determines the way it is investigated. In this respect it is useful to consider how the application for the funding of this research project posed the question. Under the heading 'Plan of Investigation' it stated:

> "Much previous research into smoking has been cross-sectional surveys of the social and psychological correlates of the phenomenon. The smoker was conceived of as a passive individual who responded by smoking when exposed to such stimuli as 'peer pressure' or 'positive beliefs about smoking' both of which were considered discrete measureable entities. The inadequacy of this approach is perhaps best illustrated by the general failure of the various anti-smoking programmes which have been based upon its evidence". (A recent review by Reid (1985) comments on the increasing effectiveness of contemporary anti-smoking campaigns).

> "The original Derbyshire survey of children's smoking behaviour attempted to overcome the limitations of a cross-sectional analysis by using a longitudinal approach. This

4

survey has produced a wealth of information about the background of smoking and its deleterious consequences. Despite this it does not completely answer the crucial question: why do children, or any group of people smoke? To answer this question and more specifically to identify those risk factors amenable to change requires a different approach".

"Recently social scientists have begun to develop an alternative methodology based upon a conception of man as a self-conscious actor who is not only aware of what he is doing but can give 'accounts' of his action (Harre and Secord, 1972). While it is agreed that the content of such accounts should not be accepted uncritically they can still provide us with an insight into the meaning of social behaviour ... Smoking should not be considered a neutral behaviour pattern emitted by passive individuals in the presence of certain stimuli but rather a social act which can have a variety of meanings in different situations. The task of the social psychologist is to identify the dimensions of these different meanings and situations".

The aim of the study that developed was two-fold:

1. to develop an understanding of the context-dependent meanings attributed to smoking by young adults;

2. to assess the extent to which such social contextual factors explained the popularity of smoking among this age group.

While the actual detail of the study changed as it unfolded the extent to which these two aims were achieved form the substance of the findings reported in this book. Before proceeding to present these findings it is useful to briefly outline the character of smoking in Britain today.

1.2   The extent of smoking in Britain today

Before the invention of the cigarette the smoking of tobacco was an occasional and largely male activity. The development of cigarette manufacturing at the close of the 19th century revolutionised tobacco use. In the atmosphere of rapid social change and consumerism which has typified Western society since the turn of the century the prevalence of cigarette smoking grew rapidly. By 1948 approximately two thirds of adult males in Britain smoked regularly (Lee, 1976) although since then the proportion has decined steadily. Historically, smoking has been less popular among women. However, after the Second World War more and more women adopted smoking such that by the beginning of the 1960s approximately 45% of adult females smoked.

An overall decline in the prevalence of smoking followed the mounting evidence linking smoking with ill-health. In 1952 Richard Doll and Bradford Hill published their famous study of mortality among British doctors. In this they implicated smoking as a major risk factor in the development of lung cancer. This was followed by an avalanche of studies linking smoking not only with lung cancer but with a variety of other diseases.

In 1962 the Royal College of Physicians published their first report on the health hazards of smoking. This led to some action by the government to curb the prevalence of smoking. For example, in 1965 the advertising of cigarettes on television was banned and in 1971 a health warning was placed on cigarette packets. In the past decade smoking has become more unpopular. According to the most recent estimates provided by the General Household Survey (O.P.C.S., 1985) the prevalence of smoking in Britain had declined by 1984 to 36% of adult males and 33% of adult females.

However, these overall figures conceal the social class disparity in the secular trend in the prevalence of smoking. Whereas in the early sixties there was little difference in the smoking behaviour of different social classes ten years later a clear social class gradient was apparent with smoking being much more popular among unskilled workers than among professionals. Today, this social class difference in the prevalence of smoking is cited as one of the reasons for the substantial social inequalities in health in Britain (Morris, 1979).

Accompanying the general decline in the prevalence of smoking among adults there has been a change in the public acceptability of the practice. Surveys have shown that most adults now agree that smoking should be restricted in public places (e.g., Marsh and Matheson, 1983).

Despite these apparent changes in attitude as assessed by questionnaire smoking still remains embedded in our society, and especially in certain sections of our society, as an accepted social practice among adults. The tobacco industry has developed on extremely sophisticated and unrelenting campaign to maintain this social acceptability of their extremely dangerous product. In 1984 they spent £41 million on the advertising of cigarettes alone with a further £8.5 million being spent on cigars and at least £6.5 million on pipe tobacco (see A. S. H. (N. Ireland)). In addition, because of the increasing restrictions on the direct advertising of their product the tobacco industry now spends an equally large sum of money on less obvious forms of promotions such as the sponsorship of sporting and cultural events. It is within this societal context of smoking being officially defined as a dangerous substance but one which is widely available and accepted that the young person develops.

Cigarettes enter the experience of children at an early age. According to Baric (1979) three out of four children are aware of cigarettes before they reach the age of five, whether or not their parents smoke. Many of these young children have handled cigarettes and played with them in their games. Indeed, a few have actually tried to smoke a lighted cigarette, sometimes with parental encouragement. During their primary school years many more children try to smoke. According to a survey conducted in Sheffield in 1978 as many as 40% of 10 year old boys and 28% of 10 year old girls reported having had at least a few puffs of a cigarette (Murray, Swan and Enock , 1981). In a national survey of 11 to 16 year olds Dobbs and Marsh (1983) found that in England and Wales 53% of the boys in their sample who had ever smoked and 35% of the girls had done so by the age of 11 years.

However, it is during adolescence that smoking becomes a regular rather than an experiemtnal practice. An earlier report of the longitudinal survey (Murray et al., 1983) showed that the prevalence of regular smoking (at least 1 cigarette a week) rose from 6% of boys and 3% of girls at 11 - 12 years to 26% of boys and 28% of girls at 15 - 16 years.

Comparison of the estimates obtained in the Derbyshire study between 1974 and 1978 with those obtained in the more recent national survey conducted by the Office of Population Censuses and Surveys in 1982 (Dobbs and Marsh, 1983) suggests that there may have been a change in the prevalence of smoking in the last decade.

Table 1   Secular change in the prevalence of adolescent smoking
          (1974 - 1982)

	Boys		Girls	
	1974(a)	1982(b)	1974(a)	1982(b)
11 - 12 years	6%	1%	3%	0%
15 - 16 years	26%	26%	23%	29%

     (a) Banks et al (1978)   (b) Dobbs and Marsh (1983)

The figures for Derbyshire (1974) and for England and Wales (1982) given in Table 1 suggest that there has been a decline in the prevalence of smoking among 11 - 12 year old boys and girls, little change in the prevalence among 15 - 16 year olds boys but an increase in the prevalence among 15 - 16 year old girls. This reversal in the sex difference in the prevalence of smoking such that older girls are more likely to smoke than boys of the same age agrees with the estimates provided in other recent surveys (e.g., Morgan, Eiser, Budd, Gamage and Gray, 1986).

Earlier experimentation with cigarettes increases the likelihood of smoking when older. In Derbyshire, two thirds of the few who were regular smokers at 11 - 12 years continued to be regular smokers four years later. Only nine percent of non-smokers adopted regular smoking within the following four years. However, only 4% of the 15 - 16 year olds who smoked regularly had been regular smokers at 11 - 12 years while 26% of them had not even tried a cigarette then and a further 40% had only tried a cigarette once (Murray et al, 1983). These figures emphasise the importance of adolescence as the period when experimentation with cigarettes is transformed into a regular practice for a large number of young people.

1.3 'Risk factors' for smoking during adolescence

Epidemiological surveys have identified a variety of social and psychololgical factors which are associated with adolescent smoking. The Derbyshire Smoking Study was a development upon

7

these surveys in that it looked at relationships over time and so was able to identify certain factors which predicted later smoking behaviour among adolescents. These predictions are based upon statistical relationships between one operationally defined variable and another. The meaning of such relationships is not always apparent and depends upon the perspective of the researcher. Despite such problems acquaintance with these predictor variables does enable us to 'set the scene' within which smoking occurs during adolescence. The main risk factors have frequently been grouped into four categories: family, friends, school and psychological factors.

(a)   Family
A strong positive association was found to exist between adolescent smoking practices and those of their parents (Murray , Kiryluk and Swan , 1985). This relationship was sex-linked such that 11 - 12 year old boys whose fathers smoked and 11 - 12 year old girls whose mothers smoked were especially at risk to be smokers themselves for years later. The longitudinal nature of the study allowed examination of change. This revealed that when the parents changed their smoking behaviour the risk of their children smoking altered accordingly. The clear sex-linking in this relationship between parents' and children's smoking suggests that to many adolescents the uptake of smoking is part of the process of becoming adult as modelled by the same sex-parent.

Having siblings who smoked also increased the risk of the adolescents adopting smoking (Murray et al., 1983). However, this relationship was not as strong as that between parents and children. It is possible that the apparent relationship between sibling's smoking practices is a reflection of parents' smoking practices.

The study also showed that during adolescence the parents became more permissive regarding their children smoking. It was suggested that this change in parental attitude reflected the fact that parents gradually relinquish control over their children during adolescence. It may well be that while many parents would prefer if their children did not smoke and restrict smoking among younger children they appear less ready to restrict smoking among older children.

Family structure was also found to be related to the uptake of smoking. Both children and parents in one-parent families were more likely to smoke. It was suggested that smoking may be a symptom of higher levels of stress within these families. Further, boys whose fathers were not at home and girls whose mothers were not at home were particularly at risk. This may have been because these children were attempting to fill the role of the missing same-sex parent. They may have adopted smoking as a means of coping with the responsibilities of this adult role or as a means of symbolically acquiring the attributes of the missing parent.

(b)   Friends
Research has consistenly found that children are more likely to smoke if their friends smoke. The Derbyshire study confirmed that early friendship with smokers increased the risk of later

smoking among adolescents (Murray et al, 1983). Interestingly this relationship only reached significance among boys from manual households among whom group membership is particularly important (Clarke, Hall, Jefferson and Roberts, 1984)

Traditionally this finding has been interpreted as indicating that young non-smoking children were being corrupted by their smoking peers. There was little consideration given to the alternative explanation that these children actively participated in the 'corruption'. In discussing alternative explanations, Eiser (1981) suggested that one reason the non-smoker adopts smoking is so as to identify with a valued group and to distinguish himself from members of another group: '... individuals do not simply yield to groups: they seek membership in groups and, through such membership, a sense of positive social identity. Conformity within a group can imply distinctiveness from other groups, and such distinctiveness can be highly valued'. This alternative perspective was apparent in our study of smoking among young adults.

The character of social relationships in early adolescence was also found to predict later smoking behaviour. Young adolescents who had friends of the opposite sex were more likely to adopt smoking than those with same-sex friends or no friends at all. This relationship was particularly apparent among girls. During adolescence girls tend to associate with boys older than themselves. Smoking may appear particularly valuable to them as a means of appearing adult and sophisticated (Bewley and Bland, 1978) or of attaining equality with their boy friends (Jacobson, 1986).

In addition, 11 - 12 year olds who engaged in a variety of social activities were more likely to adopt smoking than were those who preferred a more single lifestyle. This illustrates that smoking emerges in social interaction with one's peers rather than in isolation.

(c)   School
associated with smoking among adolescents. The Derbyshire study found a strong relationship between teachers' smoking practices and those of 11 - 12 year old boys (Bewley et al., 1979). Although a common factor may explain the smoking behaviour of teachers and pupils it is possible that the pupils model their smoking behaviour on that of their teachers. Subsequent longitudinal analyses found that while there was no relationship between boys' smoking behaviour and that of their teachers, 18 - 19 year old girls were more likely to smoke if their female teachers had smoked. It was suggested that boys may model their behaviour on that of teachers during early adolescence while girls do so in later adolescence (Murray, Kiryluk and Swan, 1984).

Other school characteristics were found to predict later smoking behaviour among adolescents. It was found that the prevalence of smoking was significantly higher among those boys who had attended schools which were single-sex, non-denominational, or which had a parent-teacher association, no health education, no female teachers, or whose head teacher smoked cigarettes. Among girls the prevalence of smoking was higher if they had attended a school which did not have compulsory school uniform, health education or specific anti-smoking education.

It was suggested that an explanation for these relationships lay in the role the school played in developing sex differences in the adolescents. The traditional male role includes such characteristics as competitiveness and independence which, if exaggerated, lead to rule-breaking and risk-taking. On the other hand, the traditional female role emphasises conformity and caution. During adolescence social norms and expectations detail the dimensions of these characteristics. Teachers' expectations play their part in this process of the development of sex roles.

In those all boys schools with no female staff social norms may accentuate aspects of the male role. This in turn may increase the risk of smoking among boys. An earlier study of 12 year olds found that a majority of both boys and girls described the smoker as a 'trouble maker' and as 'liking to do forbidden things' - the very attributes of the exaggerated male role (Bewley and Bland, 1971).

(d) Psychological factors
Specific attitudes and beliefs have frequently been identified as important risk factors in the development of smoking. In cross-sectional analyses of the Derbyshire study (Murray and Cracknell, 1980) adolescents who smoked were found to hold positive attitudes to smoking and to underestimate the health hazards of smoking. During adolescence the attitudes towards smoking by both smokers and non-smokers were found to become more positive. Conversely, they also became more aware of the health hazards of smoking.

In longitudinal analyses of the study (Murray et al , 1983) 11 - 12 year olds who held favourable attitudes to smoking and rejected the short-term health hazards were more likely than other adolescents to adopt smoking subsequently. However, these relationships did not reach significance for boys and only the latter reached significance for girls. This was probably a result of the character of the statistical analyses which did not consider the changes in attitudes and beliefs during adolescence.

1.4 Social psychological explanations for the development of smoking

While epidemiological surveys have provided a wealth of detail about the characteristics of young smokers and about the situations in which they smoke their methodology has tended to reify smoking. Smoking has been considered a fixed individual characteristic rather than an ongoing social psychological process. The epidemiological evidence cited has supported this model by referring to specific social and psychological factors which 'predict' the smoker.

The comments of Day (1982) concerning the medical approach to the study of post-natal depression are apposite in identifying the inadequacies of the epidemiological approach to the study of smoking. Day claimed that the traditional positivist methodology of medical science has reified depression as a static fixed entity. This approach 'rests on not only the acceptance of a pre-given clinical entity, but also on an implicit view of people as separate from the society that constitutes them and as passive entities on which chemical and\or social forces or factors can and do act to produce more or less specific effects in the individual'.

The alternative she poses is to view illness 'not as a passive deviation', but rather as an attempt to deal with contradictions in a particular way'. In the same way, smoking can be viewed as a means of dealing with the contradictions in one's life. This is not, of course, to deny the importance of certain fixed social and psychological factors which increase the risk of someone adopting smoking but to understand why a particular individual adopts smoking requires an understanding of the personal world of the young person.

A small attempt to achieve this was made in the original Derbyshire study. This was done by analysing the comments made by the adolescents on their questionnaires (Murray, 1984). The findings suggested that smoking was used by some adolescents in the construction of different identities. Erikson (1968) has suggested that during adolescence the young person experiments with a range of new identities. The actual character of the identity preferred will be conditioned by the ideal adult model available to his or her sex and social class. The adolescent can use various props to indicate this new identity. For example, the adolescent can change his clothing or hairstyle. Smoking was another means of indicating to others a particular identity.

An important component of identity formation is the negotiation of independence by the adolescent. According to Brehm (1965), a means of asserting our freedom is to defy authority. For some adolescents the adoption of behaviour practices condemned by authority, e.g., smoking, is part of their independence negotiation. This antipathy towards official restrictions was apparent in many of the comments made by the adolescents, both smokers and non-smokers. For example, one teenage boy wrote:

"If you want to smoke then you can if you like. What you do with your private life is your own concern, it should not be controlled by others but left to the individual (...) If you want to smoke then you should be allowed to. Life is what you make it, not what is made for you".

A vitally important component of adolescent identity is sexual identity. The adoption of smoking seemed to be used by many of the adolescents to indicate sexual maturity. Unfortunately, for girls this could sometimes be interpreted as a sign of promiscuity. For example, one non-smoking girl wrote:

"One girl I know (not a friend) she smokes over 30 a day. She is a flirt and goes out every night and smokes with her boyfriend as well as having sexual intercourse."

These few comments illustrate the value of investigating smoking from the perspective of the participants.

A more detailed attempt to understand the adolescent's world was conducted by Marklund (1979). In an attempt to understand why they adopt smoking she interviewed a sample of 80 teenagers both individually and in groups. She used the interview technique in preference to the traditional questionnaire survey which she argued forced children to think in an artifically logical manner:

"When children are requested in a school environment to answer questions in a questionnaire, they use their logical reasoning and reply as sensibly and possibly as frankly to the questions as they can. They have learnt that this is the way to behave in school. They sit alone and wonder how they would behave in a situation which the questionnaire, at best, outlines for them.

But the actual smoking occurs in a completely different environment. Surrounded by one's friends out of school, it is no longer the logical ability to reason which is the most important. The aim of being together is to have fun, to think of something to do, to experience excitment. The rules of being together are decided on other grounds, and partly by people other than those who decide the rules for classroom behaviour".

Detailed analysis of these interviews revealed developmental changes in the way adolescents view smoking. Before they reach adolescence, Marklund noted, most children have a distinctively negative view of smoking. This attitude was 'based both on knowledge of the harmful effects as well as a personal opinion that smoking is stupid and sickening'. At this age few of the children had had much direct experience of smoking.

On entry to adolescence the young people, while still having a generally negative view of smoking, begin to be influenced by conflicting norms regarding the acceptability of smoking. This is the age when experimentation with smoking becomes more widespread. Marklund noted that among 13 year olds 'smoking is part of socialising in certain circles but it doesn't seem to mean much in itself'. The value of smoking was only apparent when considered within its social context.

Another interview study of smoking among young people was that conducted by the French Committee on Health Education (1985). They conducted 44 non-directive interviews with young people aged 8 - 16 years. Careful analysis of these interviews revealed that the young people seemd to have a wide variety of social and individual 'motivations for smoking'. The report noted that 'the most striking thing about smoking is its enormous versatility, the fact that not only does it have a great number of objectives but also that these can be widely contradictory'.

The report also outlined four stages in the process of starting smoking. The first stage is pre-adolescence and is one of general hostility towards smoking. The practice is rejected by children bcause of (a) the painful effects on the senses, (b) its harmful effects on health (c) its addictiveness, (d) it is seen as a pollutant, and (e) it is seen as absurd.

In early adolescence (11 - 13 years) experimentation with smoking begins. This is described as 'the stage of forbidden games'. The following two years is 'the stage of mimicry'. Finally smoking becomes more integrated in the final stage 'when the need is internalised'.

In describing these stages the report made the following important point:

"It is important to stress that throughout this process the children are aware of what is happening and display the utmost lucidity. Not one of then is unaware of the falseness of his attmept at being taken for an adult, or of the danger he runs. But all that remains at the back of the mind, is that specific motivations to smoke are much stronger'.

1.5 Smoking among young adults

Smoking practices are not fixed by the time the adolescent leaves secondary school. Evidence suggests that the uptake of smoking continues into early adulthood. According to the Derbyshire study (Murray et al., 1983) 26% of 15 - 16 year old boys and 23% of 15 - 16 year old girls were smoking regularly in 1978. However, according to the General Household Survey (O.P.C.S., 1983) 35% of 16 - 19 year old men and 33% of 16 - 17 year old women smoked regularly in that year. These prevalence figures rose to 45% and 43% among 20 - 24 year old men and women respectively. This would suggest that regular smoking develops among many young people in late adolescence and early adulthood.

According to Levinson and his colleagues (Levinson, 1978) this period is crucial for the establishment of a mature identity and behavioural routines. They conducted intensive biographical interviews with a sample of forty men aged between 35 and 45 years. This investigation was strongly influenced by the earlier theoretical work of Erikson (1968) on human development. Although the study was limited by it's concentration on the development of men Levinson felt that many of the experiences described were similar for women.

The period of entering adulthood they termed the novice phase. This consists of a sequence of three distinct periods : early adult transition (17 - 22 years), entering the adult world (22 - 28 years), and the age 30 transition (28 - 33 years). Each of these periods has it's own particular characteristics. The study reported in this book was an investigation of the smoking practices of young people during the first period of early adult transition.

According to Levinson (1978) the period of early adult transition has two major tasks. "One task is to terminate the adolescent life structure and leave the pre-adult world and his place in it ... The second task is to make a preliminary step into the adult world : to explore it's possibilities, to imagine oneself as a participant in it, to make and test some tentative choices before fully entering it." The study reported will consider the meaning of smoking to young adults within the framework of their attempts to achieve these tasks within

13

different social contexts.

The study was conducted in two stages. The first involved detailed interviews with a sample of young adults. The second stage was based upon a survey of a large number of young adults. Each of these stages is described separately in the following two parts. The final part sumarizes the main findings and discusses the consequences of them for the development of measures to reduce the prevalence of smoking.

1.6   Summary

Despite the substantial scientific evidence linking smoking with ill-health many people continue to smoke. Previous studies designed to explain the continuing popularity of smoking , especially among young people, have been limited in their approach. They have provided comprehensive information about the extent and character of the phenomenon but provided only limited explanation of it. The study reported here is concerned with providing an introduction to the social dimension of smoking among young adults.

PART II
THE INTERVIEW STUDY

2 Design of the interview study

2.1 Introduction

The method of investigation preferred in any research carries within it implicit assumptions about the character of the issue concerned. In the social sciences the various methods of investigation are predicated upon a variety of assumptions about what is involved in being human. Discussion and argument about this issue has, of course, been the subject of philosophical speculation for centuries. With the rise of the positivist approach to science it was thought that such speculation was futile and that value free methods of inquiry would provide an objective view of man. Contemporary social scientists are not so certain about the power of the positivist approach.

Hollis (1977) suggests that there are two dominant models of man which guide empirical research within the social sciences. The first he termed Plastic Man which was the preferred model of those investigators who viewed human nature as passive. "Plastic Man is a natural creature in a rational world of cause and effect". This model underlines the traditional approach to the study of smoking which strove to identify those objectively discernable properties of the individual and his situation which caused him to smoke. According to this model, the smoker "behaves predictably in given conditions and can be manipulated by engineering apt conditions".

The second model was Autonomous Man which is preferred by those who conceive of human nature as being active. Autonomous Man has "some species of substantial self" which guides has actions towards others. Further, living within a social world, his "social action can only be understood as the rational expression of intention within rules". Adopting this model for a smoker implies that smoking is a meaningful action when considered within its social context. This is not to deny that the pharmacologic properties of nicotine do not play an important role in maintaining smoking. Indeed, this has been the subject of substantial research initiative (see Royal College of Physicians, 1983).

17

The research reported here concentrates on exploring the more neglected area of the meaning of smoking to young adults from the perspective of Autonomous Man. In doing so it is assuming that smoking is a social action over which the smoker exerts a certain degree of control. The method preferred in the first part of the project was the interview.

2.2 The interview as an approach

The approach of interviewing people is one which has a long tradition in sociology and social anthropology but one which has tended to be dismissed in psychology as being unscientific. Attempts to rehabilitate this technique within social psychology were considerably strengthened by the work of Harre and Secord (1972). They began by defining what they termed an 'anthropomorphic' model of man which is somewhat similar to Hollis' Autonomous Man. One of the distinguishing characteristics of such a man is that he is 'aware (in a weak sense) of what he is doing' and is 'capable of saying what he is up to'. In accepting such a model of man the social psychologist should be prepared to accept that 'the things that people say about themselves and other people should be taken seriously as reports of data relevant to the explanation of behaviour'. Indeed 'it is through reports of feelings, plans, intentions, beliefs, reasons and so on that the meanings of social behavior and the rules underlying social acts can be discovered'. In subsequent empirical work Harre and his colleagues (Marsh, Rosser and Harre, 1980) demonstrated the value of this approach in explaining the behaviour of a particular group of people, viz. football supporters.

The aim of this part of the research project was to collect 'accounts' from young adults about their social and working lives and the role of smoking within these contexts. These 'accounts' were then subjected to critical scrutiny to reveal the meaning of smoking to the young adults and the rules underlying its usage in various social contexts.

2.3 Study sample

A town in Derbyshire which was considered to be representative of the study area as a whole was chosen. The town selected has a population of approximately 30,000. It is an industrial town near the larger cities of Derby and Nottingham to which many of the inhabitants go for shopping and recreation. The main industries are textile and light engineering which are currently in a state of decline.

There are two secondary schools in the town, both of which took part in the original survey. One of these was a comprehensive school throughout the survey while the other changed from being a grammar school to being a comprehensive during the study period. Both schools were mixed sex and non-denominational.

Information was available from the original survey records on the parental social class and smoking behaviour of the cohort members who attended these schools between 1974 and 1978. Using this information a stratified sample was selected ensuring examples of smokers and non-smokers, males and females and a variety of different social class backgrounds. Some individuals whose parents' social class records were incomplete were also included in the sample.

A total of 88 individuals were contacted of whom 49 finally took part in the interview. All 88 were approached by letter and asked for their assistance. Twenty eight agreed immediately and a further 21 agreed subsequently. Table 2.2 gives some details of those interviewed. Of the remaining 37 young people written to, 15 were not approached for an interview, 14 were not traced, 7 refused to participate and 1 had died.

Table 2.1 Details of those interviewed

	Total	Smokers	Non-smokers	Ex-smokers
Females	21	9	11	1
Males	28	13	13	2
Total	49	22	24	3

2.4 The interviews

The interviews took place in the participants' homes except in the case of one young woman who elected, without reason, to be interviewed in the researchers' office. The interview atmosphere was generally informal with the participant or their parents often providing tea. Indeed, having answered questions on smoking almost annually for ten years many of the young adults were keen that they contributed fully to the study. In some cases the interviews took place in the presence of other family members who sometimes contributed to the discussion. This was not considered a disruption but rather a contribution to the informal atmosphere which, it was felt, encouraged more detail.

All the interviews were conducted by the first two authors (MM and LJ). The average length of time taken to conduct an interview was one hour. However, several lasted much longer and a few were quite brief. The interviews were recorded on a mini-cassette which was unobstrusive and did not seem to upset any of the participants.

The interview structure did not follow a set format but rather varied depending upon the direction of the discussion. The main themes covered in the interviews were the young adults' homelife, work, social life and health concerns and how smoking related to each of these.

2.5 Analysis of interviews

The tape-recordings were transcribed **in toto.** The transcripts were then subjected to repeated readings by the interviewers who discussed with each other their content and so helped to clarify particular aspects of the interviews. The following chapters summarise their interpretation of these interviews. It is not intended to present a comprehensive model of the causes of smoking in this age group but rather to reveal the meaning of smoking to young adults by allowing them to speak for themselves. Admittedly, certain theoretical notions influence the presentation of any data. Besides the work of Levinson(1978), we were influenced by the broad perspective provided by the work of Willis (1977), Corrigan (1979), Dorn (1984) and Griffin (1985) all of whom have conducted intensive investigations of the lives of young people.

In addition, we were inspired by the work of Goffman (1963) on interpersonal rituals and, in particular by his conceptualisation of the concepts of deference and demeanour. He defined deference as "a symbolic means by which appreciation is regularly conveyed to a recipient of this recipient" and are "ways in which an actor celebrates and confirms his relationship to a recipient". Demeanour was that aspect of the actor's behaviour which conveyed to the other person that the actor is "a person of certain desirable or undesirable qualities". In the following chapters it will become apparent that smoking is an important means of displaying deference and demeanour. Indeed, this was predicted by Goffman, viz.

> "If an individual is to act with proper demeanor and show proper deference, then it will be necessary for him to have areas of self-determination. He must have an expendable supply of the small indulgences which his society employs in its idiom of regard - such as cigarettes to give, chairs to provide, food to proffer, and so forth".

Finally, we were also aware of the work of Tajfel and his colleagues (Tajfel, Flament, Billig and Bundy, 1971) who have developed a sophisticatd understanding of the process of social interaction within and between groups. Their ideas are discussed in the conclusion.

20

3 Smoking at home

3.1 Introduction

According to Levinson's (1978) conceptionalisation of adult development the period of early adult transition presents two major tasks - leaving the pre-adult world and taking preliminary steps into the adult world. A major component of the first task is separating from the family of origin. The efforts of the young people in our investigation to accomplish this task was a central theme in the interviews.

Levinson (1978) identified both internal and external aspects of the process of separation. The former involved moving out of the family home, becoming financially less dependent and entering new roles and living arrangements in which one is more autonomous and responsible. The internal aspects involved differentiation between self and parents, greater psychological distance from the family, and reduced emotional dependency on parental support and authority. All of these aspects were apparent in our interviews.

Table 3.1 summarizes the current living situations of the young people interviewed. Two thirds were still living with their parents. Of the remaining third, roughly one half (2 males and 6 females) had married and set up their own homes. The others were either at college, had joined the forces or in the case of one young man, had simply left home to live with friends.

Table 3.1 Current living situation

	Male		Female	
	Smokers	Non-smokers	Smokers	Non-smokers
Parental Home	9	11	5	7
Married	2	-	2	4
Other	2	4	2	1

In the subsequent sections we will consider in some more detail, not only the current living situations of the young people, but also their homelife in childhood and adolescence, their plans for the future and how all of these relate to smoking.

3.2 Growing up

The young people grew up in a variety of different family types which could crudely be dichotomized as authoritarian and democratic. Their reaction to the different types of parental discipline varied. Some young women who had been reared in strict homes recalled their upbringing favourably. Katherine who did not smoke, thought greater discipline at home could reduce smoking among children:

> "[I] think its important to conduct ourselves properly. (....) I think its got a lot to do with how you're brought up, whats been hammered into you from when you were little and knowing how to behave and getting hit at the right time and things. Discipline definitely. My sister and I were brought up pretty strictly and I think its really, really helped now and we appreciate it.
>
> Katherine, non-smoker

However, other young women rebelled against their parents' attempts to enforce discipline. During adolescence they reported conflict with parents about the extent of independence allowed:

> "...towards the end of the sixth form I really wanted to get away. They were quite good. They didn't sort of put many restrictions on me but we didn't get on very well for quite a while."
>
> Alison, smoker

> "We had our ups and downs but, y'know, it was like everybody else. We had major arguments. Y'know how it is when you're growing up (....) I mean, my last year at school was really terrible."
>
> Christine, smoker

These young women smoked. But so too did some young women who came from the more democratic homes and who reported little conflict during adolescence:

> "They've never really stopped me from doing anything I wanted to."
>
> Vicki, smoker

> "I've always had an independent life. My parents have never...I've always been allowed to go out and, as I said before, I've always been allowed to have boyfriends."
>
> Tracey, smoker

One of the few young men to recall his earlier family life was a smoker. During adolescence his homelife was rather easy-going:

> "They were not that strict.   Even   me   real Dad wasn't that strict."
>
> Ron, smoker

Although limited evidence was available area it would seem that the influence of family life cannot be considered in isolation from the wider social context. For example, the adolescents' involvement in certain activities outside the home may or may not bring them into conflict with their parents. For some young people smoking may then become a symbol of their struggle for independence in this conflict situation.

Certain family events had a disruptive influence on the homelife of the young people while they were growing up. The most important seemed to be the loss of a parent either through divorce or death. The former may be more disruptive for children. One young woman, Valerie, felt that the experience of her parents' break-up and divorce was so traumatic that she refused to discuss it. She smoked.

The death of a parent seemed to be accepted with more equanimity. Debbie, recalled her youth:

> "It wasn't bad (....) but there were restrictions all round (....) my Dad died, I think I were going on for 13."
>
> Debbie, non-smoker

However, there were certain consequences of this death. Debbie suggested that she had added responsibilities. It is possible that had the deceased parent been of the same sex these responsibilities would have been even greater and similarly her risk of adopting smoking (see section 1.3).

The expected relationship between increased role responsibilities as a result of the death of a same-sex parent and increasing risk of smoking was not apparent among the young men. Tim mentioned that to an extent he had taken on the role of head of household after the death of his father and felt protective towards his mother:

> "Since my father died 6 years ago I can imagine what it's like to lose your husband (....) I can imagine her being hurt (...) I resent her working all the time. She keeps her mind on work. I resent that. I say go out and enjoy yourself socially."
>
> Tim, non-smoker

As well as his concern for his mother   Tim took responsibility for his younger sister. However, Tim did not smoke.

John, another young man, hinted at how the death of his father was an emotional blow to him:

> "My Dad died when I was 10. I don't [miss him] now, I
> did then."
>
> John, smoker

However, there was little suggestion that John had adopted
the head of household role after his father's death. He did
smoke. Thus, although the death of a parent may increase the
risk of an adolescent adopting smoking the reason for this is
complex.

3.3 Current family life

After conflict with parents during adolescence most of the
young people had now reached an accommodation with them over
their activities. The young men reported a few arguments but
these seemed to be of little consequence:

> "...we get on quite well, really, the family. We argue
> (....) and stuff, but its only natural, innit?"
>
> Ken, non-smoker

A few mentioned the occasional restrictions:

> "Me Mum (...) she's the boss in the house (...)
> Occasionally I get, 'Don't be late, don't do this ,
> don't do that.' But that's me mother, y'know."
>
> Guy, non-smoker

Only Mick felt that these restrictions had to be taken
seriously:

> "I find it alright as long as I don't - I have to
> be in by a certain time every night if I'm going
> anywhere (...) If I'm going out I'm always back by that
> certain time. I'm always dead on time. I rush to get
> back by that time".
>
> Mick, ex-smoker

A few young men did mention current conflict at home. These
tended to be non-smokers:

> "Me mother (....) she governs at home. If she
> doesn't like something that's happening in the
> house its not worth like arguing about it. Keep
> your head down (....) I'm used to living with
> it. It gets on me nerves at times, then we have
> blazing rows (....) But there's no two ways about
> it really, it's if you can't really live
> with it you'd have to move out, like my sisters."
>
> Roger, non-smoker

It was as if the non-smokers were experiencing the family
rows over independence which the smokers had experienced
much earlier in adolescence.

The unemployed men reported a general 'getting in the way'
problem with their parents as a result of being around all day:

"We have these big arguments sometimes. Usually about each other usually. 'I'm sick of you doing this, I'm sick of you doing that' We're both at home during the day, that's why I made this place [his room] me own in a way. It keeps me out of the road like."

John, smoker

The young women were less likely to report current family conflict. Katherine was the only one:

"We're always having arguments, especially Mum and myself."

Katherine, non-smoker

It was much more usual for them to report an improvement in family relations:

"We always argued, all of us, me brother and me and me Mum, me step-dad. Ever since he's gone there's hardly been any argument at all."

Lisa, smoker

When they had problems, say at work, the young people often discussed them with their parents in an adult-to-adult manner:

"If I got any problems I'll always talk to me Mum and Dad or me girlfriend (....) If I have any problems that's where I go. I've got very understanding parents."

Sam, smoker

Sam came from a working class family. On the other hand, Vicki who came from a middle class home had not yet established a comfortable relationship with her parents such that she could discuss her problems with them:

"I keep [problems] to meself. I don't say anything, or very rarely. I just, well, I take (....) each day as it comes (....) I think, I'll worry about it when it comes and then as soon as it comes its over with then. You just laugh to get through it."

Vicki, smoker

It seemed that while in working class homes the conflict concerning independence was completed by the time the children left school, in middle class homes it was often the reverse. Thus, smoking as a symbol of the struggle for independence would only become of value to middle class youth during this period whereas for working class youth it was such a symbol several years earlier.

3.4 Parental expectations

An earlier analysis of the Derbyshire study (Murray, Swan, Johnson and Bewley, 1983) found that children who viewed their

College of St. Francis Library
Joliet, Illinois

parents as being generally unconcerned about their children's social activities and their future behaviour were more likely to adopt smoking. A similar relationship was apparent in the interviews. Some of the non-smokers remarked upon their parents' interest in their school progress, e.g.

"They're pleased because I got all my 'O' levels and 'A' levels. They're very interested in academic success."

Judith, non-smoker

"I think he's quite content. Every father likes his son to do a lot better than what he's doing, y'know, like to think that the son can do better than the father."

Tony, non-smoker

Even disappointment was interpreted as general concern:

"Perhaps I didn't do as well at school as she thought I might, although certain things I was quite good at [I was encouraged to stay on at school but] I think Mum assumed I was just going to leave."

Len, non-smoker

In general, the women were less likely to be encouraged to obtain more qualifications but this did not mean that parental interest was lacking:

"I asked my father to stay on [at school] a bit more and he wanted me to get out and work. I think he thinks I'm a bit naive about things. I think, in a way, they feel I need protecting, but I don't think that (....) I think basically they want me to be happy. I don't think they're looking in terms of being really career minded (....) They don't want me to get to the top or anything."

Katherine, non-smoker

One young woman had established herself in a profession as a nursery nurse and she felt her parents were pleased:

"I think they're very proud of the fact that...of the job I've got, y'know. They're proud of the fact I went to College and, I suppose, bettered myself."

Tracey, smoker

It is interesting to note that Tracey was the only smoker who thought her parents had high expectations for her and she went on talk of how they were disappointed in her smoking:

"My Dad said it was the biggest disappointment in his life. I'm very close to my Dad and that really came home."

Tracey, smoker

The smokers had less to say about their parents' attitude to them and if they did it was more in terms of their parents opinion of what the child had made of his or her life rather than a memory of parental encouragement to better themselves. It seemed indicative of a more independent lifestyle and sometimes a less amiable parent-child relationship. For example:

> "I think sometimes, sometimes she hates what I do. Y'know the fact that I've got a bike and I spend most of me money on bikes going out at weekends and things like that."
>
> Frank, smoker

In the earlier analyses (Murray et al, 1983) it also emerged that the children whose parents were perceived as being unconcerned about them were more involved in outside social activities. It was suggested that these children's perception of lack of parental concern led them to place a greater value on their peer group and to take less heed of any parental restrictions, such as on smoking.

Perceived parental expectations were, to an extent, reflected in the young people's views of their parents. Many young men and women were quite critical of their parents:

> "I think my Dad could have done a lot more than he has done in fact. But I think he gets into a situation where if you work any harder you're not going to get any reward for it anyway."
>
> Mick, ex-smoker

> "Me mothers never done anything really to better herself. She's only worked part-time (....) My father's always stayed as he was instead of striking out and attempting to do something."
>
> Helen, non-smoker

> "Mummy isn't at all outgoing. She likes sitting in every night watching TV whereas Daddy goes out three nights a week playing badminton, squash, and things."
>
> Katherine, non-smoker

These comments were from non-smokers. There seems to be an association between the parents making high demands on the children, including encouragement not to smoke, and the children's expression of similar standards in their criticism of their parents.

The smokers had little comment to make about their parents and what they said was generally favourable and certainly less critical:

> "I think she's done very well really. I mean she's had a hard time. Me parents got divorced when I was 7 and she brought my sister and I up single-handed really, without much help."
>
> Frank, smoker

"They think the world of my boyfriend. They always make him welcome here. They've always, always made people welcome, anybody I want to bring home"

Tracey, smoker

Such comments from the smokers could be an indication that they have been brought up in a more liberal environment where they have been allowed to make decisions. They have been allowed to set their own standards and, as a result, may be less critical of parents who have allowed them that opportunity.

3.5 Involvement in the home

The young men and women looked at the parental home with different eyes. Invariably, although to different degrees, the men used the home as a base from which to lead their wider social life and were hardly ever involved in domestic chores. It was only a few of the young women, especially the smokers, who viewed the home in a similar way and even they had domestic responsibilities:

"I'm never really in the house. I'm only in when I come home from work, sort of thing."

Vicki, smoker

"It's a bit boring being the only one, but I'm hardly here."

Jenny, non-smoker

The development of the domestic female role was apparent in some of the young women's comments:

"I do help me Mum with the housework. When I was younger I was doing mostly most of it meself. I don't have too much responsibility now 'cause there's sort of those behind me."

Mary, non-smoker

Typically there was no active role for the male in the domestic chores and this resulted in lack of interest and boredom leading to a desire to get up and go out. Again, this was especially the case for the smokers:

"[When I come home in the evening I'm] ready to go out and do something. I live a bit here, a bit at Hillside and a bit at my girlfriend's and all over (...) I never stay here at night [parents' home] I don't know why. I either go to my girlfriend's, y'know, when I've done my weight-training er ... I don't know, I get bored staying in one place, really, y'know. If there's nowt on tele I go out."

George, smoker

"Every night [I go out] I like to get out of the house y'know. It's boring here (....) I like to get out of the house 'cause I don't like being here. It's boring for me. I've got to get out of the house and meet me mates, talk to them, light a fag,

probably have a drink, walk around, talk, have some
fun, muck about. Just sitting in watching tele, I think
life's passing on by without me. I get bored. I'm
usually out till late every night, then I come in, I go
to bed, I get up, I go to work, I come home, have my
tea, and get washed and changed and then I go out and
if you wasn't here I'd be out now, you know. I'm always
out.I don't like being in the house and I'm out at the
weekend so its very rare I'm in, so I don't get
involved."

Dennis, smoker

Even when staying in, the young men felt that there was
nothing to do:

"[At home] I find I watch tele. That's all I do. Watch
tele or I go upstairs and listen to music."

Sam, smoker

The only young single man to talk specifically about
domestic responsibilities was Roger. His father was an invalid
and Roger had taken over some domestic duties. He was also a
non-smoker:

"I get clobbered to do the odd jobs, but it doesn't feel
as if its anything special. I mean, I'm not called upon
to quit College early or go out and earn (....) The
only thing that strikes me that's slightly different
from any other household is the fact that you're always
called to do the heavy jobs."

Roger, non-smoker

It would seem that the single men and women who were involved
in the home were less likely to smoke. These were the
'homebirds' who had little social life outside the home.

3.6 Parental smoking

Much previous psychological research has identified parental
smoking behaviour as a 'cause' of smoking among adolescents.
Thus it was not surprising that many of the young smokers had
parents who smoked. The sex-linking of the relationship, which
was reported earlier (see section 1.3) was apparent in some of
the comments:

"Me Dad smokes, me brother smoker, me sister don't
smoke, me Mum don't smoke (....) Me Mum don't mind [me
smoking] cause me Dad's smoked since she met him (....)
He won't pack up so she's just got used to that. So
she's seeing it with me older brothers. I've got two
older brothers, besides me, and they both smoke."

Bill, smoker

" ... there's me and me Dad, Colin and Greg smoke, but
the two women don't (...) so we smoke the house out and
they just have to put up with it."

Dennis, smoker

However, some of the young people who smoked referred to an opposite-sex parent as a model of the adult smoker. For example:

> "I think what started me smoking was seeing me Dad smoking. I thought 'Oh I wonder what its like, y'know, have a cigarette' I thought to myself 'Oh I'd like to try that, y'know."
>
> Sarah, smoker

Further, many of the young adults did not smoke although their parents smoked. There was a suggestion that in these cases the same sex parent was a light smoker:

> "Me Mum smokes quite a lot. But me Dad now and again (....) Me Mum [smokes] when she gets up in the morning and then goes through the day until she goes to bed at night. But me Dad, he may have [no] more that two a day."
>
> Terry, non-smoker

> "Me Mum smokes a lot more, I think, since she's been to work ... not excessive, perhaps six a day, something like that. Me Dad, he's cut out smoking cigarettes and mostly has a cigar (...) perhaps five at the weekend and perhaps one or two a day."
>
> Graham, non-smoker

The sight of their parents smoking actually discouraged some of the young people from smoking. This was the case with Roger:

> "... something I've always grown up to dislike because me Mum and Dad used to smoke heavily. Waking up to rooms that stank of cigarettes just makes me feel dreadful now."
>
> Roger, non-smoker

Some of the young people whose parents smoked not only did not smoke themselves, but tried to discourage their parents from smoking:

> "I keep trying to persuade my Dad not to smoke but he keeps on smoking (....) I keep pointing articles in the paper out to him (....) It has no effect."
>
> Linda, non-smoker

> "My father smokes but he always has done (...) One place he doesn't smoke that's in my car. He can do what he likes in his own but he's not smoking in mine."
>
> Helen, non-smoker

It is obvious that while parental smoking may provide a model for the adoption of smoking by the adolescent it is not automatic. Rather, whether the young person becomes a smoker depends on a variety of other factors.

3.7 Parents' reaction to early smoking

Initial experimentation with cigarettes almost always took place outside the home (Section 6.2). The reaction of parents on finding out their children smoked varied. Those who started smoking early found only minimal resistance from their parents especially if they themselves smoked. They were usually discovered smoking by their parents accidentally:

> "Let's say 14 I started smoking (....) me mates and that y'know. That's how I started (....) I was having a smoke, me Mam walked in and caught me and she saw me, went off in a huff and then when I got in the room she said 'Well you can smoke anyway'. So nothing happened and she told me about what it's bad for you and all this lot, give me a lecture. All that happened really."
>
> Ron, smoker

When Sarah was caught smoking by her mother she thought:

> "Oh they're going to kill me, y'know. I was scared stiff. But when me Mum told me Dad, me Dad wasn't very bothered at all. He said 'Well its your life, if you want to ruin it by smoking, you go ahead'. And of course, everytime it made me think but I still kept on smoking. But he said. Don't come back to me if you ever get anything like lung cancer like that (....) I don't want to know."
>
> Sarah, smoker

Those who started smoking later either deliberately smoked in front of their parents or asked permission to smoke:

> "I always remember the first time I lit up a fag in here [at home] (....) One day George [brother-in-law] just chucked me a fag and he says. 'Come on Bri, light it up'. So I just sat there and lit it up. Me Mum says. 'What are you doing with that?'. I said 'I'm smoking it'. 'Not in here you're not' (....) I said 'why not everybody else smokes in here why can't I?'. Me Dad said. 'Oh leave him, let him smoke it.' So that was that, I smoked."
>
> Brian, smoker

> "I never started smoking properly until after I'd left school and I left school in June and then in August I started smoking at home. I asked if I could smoke at home. I asked my Mum and Dad and they said Yes."
>
> Christine, smoker

All these young people came from working class homes where their parents smoked. The parent-child relationship seemed to reach an adult-adult stage earlier in these homes such that the parents tended to consider their children responsible for their decision to adopt smoking from an early age.

Peter came from a middle class home and did not adopt smoking until he was sixteen. However, he found that his parents

31

protested little. His mother smoked. When they discovered he smoked they:

> "Just went out and bought me an ashtray (....) They disapproved but they thought, I think they thought that if they didn't say anything I'd grow out of it."
>
> Peter, smoker

However, Mick who came from a middle class home where his parents did not smoke found a different reaction. His father was very strict in all matters. Although Mick did smoke for a while he soon stopped:

> "Me Dad found out and that was it (....) I felt more guilty than anything else about it. I stopped eventually I think [because of] pressure from me Dad to, y'know,
>
> Mick, smoker

Many of the non-smokers recalled their parents discouraging them from smoking:

> "'You don't want to smoke.' It was a bit odd at first, thinking, y'know, what's she on about, y'know, she's got a cigarette in her hand saying - 'Oh don't smoke' y'know, a bit confusing at first (....) but seems to work."
>
> Ken, non-smoker

> "Me Dad didn't want me to smoke ever (...) He told me its not worth smoking (...) hen you get older you realise that, you know."
>
> Jenny, non-smoker

Roger remembered his parents severely discouraging him. This did not prevent him experimenting with cigarettes but he did not become a regular smoker:

> "I was told what a dreadful thing it was [My parents] threatened me with violence if they ever caught me with cigarettes (....) I guess it must have [had an effect]. I once tried smoking when I was really young, but felt pretty awful afterwards."
>
> Roger, non-smoker

Other non-smokers remembered their parents being easy going:

> "[My parents] always said it was up to me (....) I don't think my Mum would like it if I started smoking. She's against smoking. My brother doesn't smoke. I don't think he'd ever smoke. It's always up to me."
>
> Linda, non-smoker

> [My parents] didn't really bother. They sort of said its best not to smoke."
>
> Darren, non-smoker

Overall, the comments illustrate the importance of parental attitude besides parental example in the development of smoking during adolescence. The attitude adopted by the parents were related to their own smoking behaviour and social class and also depended on when the young person started smoking.

3.8 Smoking at home

Now that they were adult, smoking in the home was viewed quite differently by these young people. Even though other family members were often smokers, cigarette smoking at home was more often than not described as a solitary occupation. Christine's description implied that smoking was something to do when bored:

> "I smoke more when I'm at home (...) because I tend to spend most of my time in front of the tele (...) and I'll sit there with me knitting and I'll have a fag on. I mean, I've not got it in my hand all the time but it'll be there in the ashtray. I mean I can go without, it doesn't bother me to go all afternoon without as long as I've got something to do. It's just if I've got nothing to do I tend to get a fag out of the packet and that's it."
>
> Christine, smoker

Others, who were more socially active, talked about smoking alone while getting ready to go out. Hilary, who spaced out her smoking at work and smoked very little in a social setting, said:

> " ...it's when I get home that I want a cigarette, I suppose. When I'm at home upstairs in my bedroom on me own and getting ready (.....) if I'm home I could smoke five while I'm getting ready to go out."
>
> Hilary, smoker

Frank only smoked occasionally at home and usually alone:

> "[At home I'll smoke] after dinner usually and if I've washed me hands, I'm dried and dressed, waiting for me hair to dry and I'll usually have one in the bedroom."
>
> Frank, smoker

Vicki had little time for smoking in the house. For her smoking was part of the process of 'getting ready':

> "I'm never really in the house. I'm only in when I come home from work, sort of thing and I'll have a fag when I'm getting ready so I don't really have time for many."
>
> Vicki, smoker

Emma only smoked in the house, never at work or socially. Although a light smoker, smoking was such a part of her life at home that she could not imagine being without a packet of cigarettes:

> "I only smoke when I get home [I don't smoke when I'm out] (....) Sometimes I can sit in this house with a packet of fags and I won't touch them. But if I haven't

33

got them there, I don't know, I feel a bit lost. Perhaps because I've done it for two years now and you feel lost without it. You get used to it."

Emma, smoker

Some of the young smokers explained how they restricted their smoking at home because of parental restrictions. Mick had even given up smoking because his father disapproved and he could not continue to smoke comfortably at home.

Nick's parents also disapproved and he restricted his smoking in front of them. Smoking was definitely a part of his social life outside home:

"I suppose people at work are older, you know, tend to be older and sort of represent me Mum and Dad. I mean I'd never smoke in front of me Mum and Dad, but in front of young people I would."

Nick, smoker

Sam restricted his smoking in his parents house. He felt he was being respectful. His parents were not against him smoking, but they disliked the side effects:

"Me Dad doesn't like smoking in the house when he's in. It gets on his chest so I don't usually smoke in the house. I'll have one or two while they're out but I don't smoke while they're in 'cause they don't like it, they don't like the smell."

Sam, smoker

Parental disapproval of their smoking was mentioned by several of the women. At this stage, however, the parents seemed resigned to the fact:

"Me Mum hates me smoking. [My husband] doesn't like me smoking but he' not as bad as me Mum."

Valerie, smoker

"I just told her [I smoked]. She [my mother] wasn't very pleased but now, you know, when we're out I just light a cigarette and (....) she won't say much, you know, she tells me to put it out."

Marion, smoker

It would seem that the lack of equitable social relations at home reduces the value of smoking to these young people. Instead, smoking becomes a solitary activity. It's value in this situation varies but it seems particularly important as a means of structuring time during periods of boredom, especially among the young people who enjoyed an active social life outside the home.

3.9 Desire for independence

All the young people expressed some desire for independence. However, although they talked about it, the prospect of leaving the family home as a young, single adult was rarely seen

as a possibility.   Cost of alternative housing   was
prohibitive even when available.   Some, especially the
smokers, strove more than others for their independence:

> "I'm looking for a flat (...) to be independent
> really (...) I'd like to live on my own but I couldn't
> afford it."
>
> Emma, smoker

> "If I had the money I'd move away but not at the moment
> cause I can't afford it (....) move away from the house.
> I'd like a place of me own.   At the moment there's no
> way I could afford it."
>
> Frank, smoker

Others seemed more reluctant to leave home, or at least
were more realistic in their plans for the future.   This
sometimes went along with a greater feeling of contentment
about living with their parents:

> "[I feel] quite independent but not as independent as
> I'd like to be. I'd sooner 'ave my own flat (...) I've
> got a very nice home here. I couldn't ask for more
> really."
>
> Tom, smoker

> "[My home life is] alright (....) I'd like my own house
> but I haven't got enough money for that at the moment
> so I'd just try and save up as quickly as I can.   Not
> that I want to get away but [I] don't want to live here
> all the time."
>
> Len, non-smoker

Hilary had spent a short time living away from home and the
financial cost of the experience led her to rationalise
her step towards marriage. It would be her only means of gaining
independence:

> "I'm alright here but I want me independence (....) I
> lived in a bedsit before but er.. it's ever so expensive
> Fourteen pounds fifty a week and there wasn't a great
> deal (....) I say I want to get married, all I want
> really is me own house, me independence."
>
> Hilary, smoker

Most young women were prepared to live with their parents.
Like Hilary, most felt that getting married was the only means
of achieving independence from the parental home.   Only two
women said they had no plans for marriage at all. This was in
complete contrast to the young men.   Only two of the single
men admitted marriage plans.

Dependence on the parents was complete in the case of
the unemployed. None talked about leaving home, whatever
family relationships were like.   Jason summed up his
dependence on his mother:

> "I don't [manage on the dole] I'm very lucky, 'cause
> my mother doesn't charge me much board."
>
> Jason, smoker

Thus the desire of the young people, especially of the young smokers, for independence, was severely constrained by economic factors. In Levinson's (1978) study a large proportion of the young men entered the armed forces or college which provided another means of breaking the financial ties with parents. These two options are discussed in the next chapter.

3.11 Married life

Six women and two men were married. The married men contrasted not only with the women but also with their single male contemporaries. Marriage had changed the extent of their social life because of the demand of domestic responsibilities:

> "We never go out down here (....) I've decorated the house and that and fetched the wood and jobs here and there in the garden and that, and that's about it."
> Ron, smoker

The home was often used as a centre for social activities:

> "I don't go out regular. I'll have a drink in. On Friday night I'll have a drink in but, you know, I wouldn't go out (....) I'll have a drink in more than I'll go out actually."
> Ron, smoker

Friends would come around and share in this arrangement as described by another married man:

> "[In the evenings we] watch tele, clean the house (....) we always have people coming round visiting."
> Bill, smoker

The fact that friends came around or dropped by emphasized the continuation, in a changed form, of these young men's social life.

All but one of the married women were mothers with young children. They spent a lot of their time at home. Some were more socially active than others. Valerie often spent her days with other young mothers and her own mother. She was a smoker:

> "We go out shopping, housework, see friends quite a lot (....) sit talking, shopping."
> Valerie, smoker

She remembered the change in her life after giving up work and getting married:

> "We've been married three years in September...when I was made redundant. I think I got pregnant not long after that. Up 'til then, me life, you know, 'til I had Cathy, me life was pretty quiet. Not a lot to do."
> Valerie, smoker

She had some difficulty adjusting to the change:

36

"Well I like it now (....) At first it took some getting used to. I couldn't get used to it at all at first (....) I used to forget to come here and I used to ride home to me Mum's from work."

Valerie, smoker

Debbie, a non-smoker, felt much more isolated. Her lack of social life was apparent:

"My sister-in-law's arranged for us to go out to a Bier Kellar tonight so I said I'd go. Make a change 'cause I haven't been out for what, nearly two years on my own. I'm going there tonight 'cause my husband's watching him...I still wish I was back at the factory, y'know, just for a bit of fun now and again 'cause usually I'm in the house 24 hours a day y'know. Probably just pop down the shops or down to me mother-in-laws which is just down the road y'see. I don't really go far."

Debbie, non-smoker

Despite these restrictions, Debbie felt content in her role as a mother and as a housewife. Commenting on the occasional times when she was sick or when she was at her part-time job, to which she took her child, she referred to the role of her husband:

"I like it actually [married life]. But I mean, different people have different opinions. I suppose if you think you've got the right one you're alright (...) 'cause my husband helps anyway. I mean, if I'm bad or say I'm at work he stops in. When I come back everything's done - me housework, me washing. He can't iron, he leaves that for me to do but everything else is done, beds, everything."

Debbie, non-smoker

It was apparent that marriage is followed by a dramatic change in the lifestyle of these young women but to a lesser extent for the young men who still continue their normal work routine and their social life, although the latter is modified. Generally, the greater the isolation caused by marriage, the less the value of smoking. This was especially the case for the young women.

3.11 Summary

The purpose of this chapter was to consider how the young people viewed their home life and their experience of smoking at home. The initial comments about early family life. He confirmed the importance of parental behaviour and attitudes in orienting the young people towards the acceptability or unacceptability of smoking.

The chapter also revealed the changing attitude of the young people towards their homelife now that they were entering early adulthood. To those who engaged in active social life what happened at home seemed of little consequence. If these young parents or other family members. In Levinson's (1978) terms, smoking seemed particularly important to those who were eager to leave the pre-adult world and to establish an adult identity separate from their parents.

The young people who had married and were now beginning to establish their own homelife spent a lot more time at home. If smoking occurred, it was often when friends visited.

4 Smoking at work

4.1 Introduction

The second major task of the period of early adult transition
(Levinson, 1978) is preparation for entry into the adult world.
At the beginning of this period "a young man's knowledge, values
and aspirations for a particular kind of adult life are rather
ambiguous and colored by private fantasies. He needs to obtain
further training and learn more about himself and the world.
Gradually he articulates his earlier fantasies and hopes into
more clearly defined options for adult living. As the transition
ends he will make firmer choices, define more specific goals and
gain a higher measure of self-definition as an adult."

Many of these characteristics were apparent in our study when
the young adults spoke about their working life. However,
whereas Levinson's work was conducted in America during a period
of high employment our study was conducted in Britain at a time
of increasingly limited job opportunities, especially for young
people. Instead of the beginnings of the smooth upward mobility
which characterised many of the men in Levinson's study, many of
the young adults in our study, both men and women, expressed
frustration at the blocking of goals and ambitions.

The sample of young people interviewed provided a good
cross-section of occupations. Table 4.1 shows that almost two
thirds of the sample were currently employed with the ratio
of manual to non-manual workers being 2:1. Just over one
tenth were unemployed but had previously held jobs and a
tenth were housewives who had also previously worked. A
further tenth were students and the remaining twentieth were in
the armed forces. The sample also provided examples of smokers
and non-smokers in all but a few of the occupational
categories.

In the following description of their working life the
emphasis will be on those young people who were currently in
full-time civilian employment with only a brief mention of

certain of the particular characteristics of members of the armed forces, students, unemployed and young mothers.

Table 4.1: Current occupation and smoking behaviour of young people interviewed

Current occupation	Male		Female	
	Smokers	Non-smokers	Smokers	Non-smokers
Manual	6	8	3	3
Non-manual	2	2	3	4
Unemployed	4	1	-	1
Student	-	3	1	1
Housewife	-	-	2	3
Forces	1	1	-	-

4.2 Preparation for work

At school few of the adolescents had clearly defined plans as to the nature of the job they would enter. Despite this it was still possible to discern sex and social class differences in their plans. Few of those from working class households seemed to have given much consideration to the possibility of further or higher education. Rather the aim was to get a secure job, to earn money and to become an adult. For boys, the specific objective which could ensure the attainment of these aims was to obtain an apprenticeship. The following comments illustrate this desire for an apprenticeship:

> "At school I said I wanted to do an apprenticeship. I didn't really know what I wanted to do at all. I still don't know really what I want to do but I'm doing it anyway".
>
> Tim, non-smoker

By obtaining an apprenticeship , these young men thought that subsequently they would be sure of regular employment and good wages. Some were a little more specific. They specified jobs for which they thought they had exhibited talent at school. For example:

> "Just done four years precision engineering (...) it was what I wanted to do basically when I left schoool. I was good at metalwork and that was about it".
>
> Brian, smoker

While Ken was somewhat more general in his choice:

> " I didn't want to work in a factory (....) I like to be outside and thats who I wanted to go in the building trade".
>
> Ken, non-smoker

40

However, for girls from working class homes entry into such skilled trades was blocked. Instead it was assumed that after school most would obtain some unskilled or semi-skilled factory or clerical work. The almost inevitability of this transition was apparent in the following comment:

"Didn't really think about it. All I thought about was working at Brown's where I'm working now (...) Ever since the fourth year 'cause we all went from school and had a look round it and, y'know, dead clean and everybody was dead friendly".

Marion, smoker

For these girls the character of the job seemed of lesser importance than the means it provided for acquiring certain valued attributes. For example, Jill described her reasons for leaving school:

"Because of money, to get to work and buy clothes and go out".

Jill, non-smoker

Admittedly some of the girls had an ambition of securing entry into one of the more male trades. However, they found this almost impossible. Marion's ambition since school had been to become a lorry driver:

"My ambition is to drive and be a long-distance lorry driver (....) I'm determined to do it"

Marion, smoker

In an effort to achieve this she had recently left her job as a textile machinist and taken a temporary job with a car-rental agency:

"... lots of driving involved. Delivering cars and collecting cars"

Marion, smoker

But she was dissatisfied with this. What she really wanted was to drive trucks, "big trucks". She was planning to take lessons to obtain a HGV licence which could help her escape from her factory job.

Similarly, Vicki, who had several clerical jobs since leaving school really wanted to be a bricklayer. At school she remembered:

"I was really mad about bricklaying.... well I still would like to be one...... I've applied every year except for this one".

Vicki, smoker

When asked why she thought it has been so difficult to obtain such a job she replied:

"Because I'm female, full stop."

Both these young women were smokers. Frustrated in their

attempts to develop their skills they may have smoked as a means of coping with a job they disliked. Vicki obviously felt she did not fit in with the other staid office workers:

> "Everybody at work is very 'holy' sort of thing - stop in at night, knitting and all that lot and I'm out every night".
>
> Vicki, smoker

The work, too, was annoying:

> "I like something, not fiddly bits of paper, something y'know, to do, y'know, results at the end sort of thing"
>
> Vicki, smoker

Similarly Marion when asked why she left a recent job replied:

> "I found myself doing nothing and, to me, just sitting there getting paid for it, I mean its nice but, y'know, I felt that I didn't do enough to earn me money."
>
> Marion, smoker

By smoking, these young women could dissociate themselves from their staid non-smoking colleagues. Smoking enabled them to identify with a more exciting world outside their present work.

The adolescents, both male and female, from middle class homes also recalled that at school their work plans were rather confused. However, most of them accepted that they would not leave school at the minimum age but would stay on. For example:

> "Soon as I started sixth form I'd no intention of getting a job after A-levels - just went straight into University".
>
> Roger, non-smoker

However, some had this steady progression to higher education blocked because of examination failure. Peter was typical:

> "Well, I did want to go to university to do various things but none of them came through because I failed them [exams] through lack of work."
>
> Peter, smoker

Now he felt his talents were being ignored. He felt frustrated and was anxiously searching for a better position.

> "I'm bored with it (...) At the moment I'm still looking round for other jobs (...) better jobs".
>
> Peter, smoker

Like Vicki and Marion, he smoked.

For those young people from middle class homes who did not plan to enter higher education, the aim was to obtain a secure and respectable office job. Katherine who had obtained a job as a bank clerk, described her feelings at school:

"I didn't know really what I wanted to do at all and as far as I was concerned I wanted a job I enjoyed and I wanted it to be a very stable job which - I was very lucky to get into the bank (...) I was just trying for sort of local jobs but I knew the bank had a bit of prestige behind it for one thing".

Katherine, non-smoker

Katherine was quite satisfied with her current work situation. She did not smoke. It seemed that those who were content with their current job were less likely to smoke.

4.3 Entry to work

Although usually eagerly anticipated, the young people sometimes found that entry to work was fraught with problems. The major problem seemed to be conflict with older workers rather than difficulty learning the actual job. Tony, an apprentice mechanic, recalled:

"At first I was a bit, didn't get on very well with people (...) just didn't sort of mix with them like, y'know... lot older and knew a lot about work and I'd just started and they expected a bit too much from me at first".

Tony, non-smoker

Many of the young women mentioned similar problems. They emphasized that the conflict tended to centre on the status of the new worker as either an adult or a child. The new workers were trying to be adult whereas the older workers continued to treat them as children. According to Emma, an unskilled machinist:

"They don't class you as adults (....) They still think they can sort of talk down to you and tell you what to do and talk to you like they would a kid".

Emma, smoker

In school the young people's social relations were largely confined within limited age-bands. Now they had to begin to understand people much older than themselves. Emma continued:

"When you get to work with them, y'know, you don't know how to treat them and you find out really (....) most of them are just big, y'know, just as childish as what you are".

Emma, smoker

In this period of rapid assimilation into adulthood the young worker felt a strong desire to conform to adult norms of behaviour. For many young people, this included adopting smoking. Alison, the only female student who smoked, recalled this experience:

"I seriously started smoking, sort of buying them, when I was working at a factory during school holidays. When I'd left school after my A levels and between coming to

university I worked in a factory and thats when I
started buying them and smoking regularly (...) It was
mostly the women who were working there - the majority
of them smoked. I think it was just the kind of right
thing to do".

Alison, smoker

Tom, an apprentice machinist, also felt the incentive to smoke
when he started work:

"The temptation was there from work 'cause lots of
blokes at work smoke, y'know. It's like there's a toilet
and they all go in there, in this corridor, all smoking.
I like to go in there to find out what's going off
like .... and they're all smoking away. I'm just sitting
there. So the temptation was there when I first started"

Tom, smoker

Two of the non-manual male workers had progressed to their
present position through part-time work while at school. Len
worked part-time in the family travel agency:

"I used to go round Saturday and work there then. Part
of the way through he said did I want to work full-time
when I left school. So I just got into that"

Len, non-smoker

Similarly Graham obtained his present job in the local
grocery store through previous experience there:

"I worked there when I was a little lad, y'know
sugar-stacking, things like that"

Graham, non-smoker

Entry into full- time work for these young men was accomplished
with relatively few difficulties. Neither of them experienced
any temptation to start smoking.

4.4 Interesting and boring jobs

Most of the young men who had succeeded in
obtaining an apprenticeship were happy in their work. For
example, Dennis who was training to be a coachbuilder said:

"The jobs interesting. I like it. I'm happy there
Its great (...) I like it".

Dennis, smoker

Those aspects of the job which particularly raised
satisfaction with work were variety in the job and the
amount of responsibility allowed. Bill, the apprentice engineer,
proudly described his job:

"On my job I have to do everything myself. I fetch the
bars. I sharpen the tools, everything I do...With other
jobs you have other people doing it for you"

Bill, smoker

While Tony, the apprentice lace mechanic said:

> "It varies, see. There's quite a few of us knitting,
> watching the machines, fixing them up and setting them
> up and there's changing the patterns on the machines and
> there's what they call warping as well.
>
> Tony, non-smoker

The desire to have a varied job in which one has
control and responsibility was evident in the decision of Ron who
gave up his job as a mechanic to become a seasonal worker in an
amusement park:

> "It's great. I love it. Beautiful (...) I'm foreman on
> a go-kart track. Well, I'm foreman of the park really -
> all the amusement park - but my job is a go-kart
> mechanic and things because we've got go-karts, petrol
> engines and, em, I'm in charge of the go-kart track, to
> run it and mend it and help with good running (...) You
> really can't tell people. They'll say: 'Oh, I wouldn't
> do that'. The money's not all that good. But its just
> that you're out in the open air all the time and it's
> really great, y'know".
>
> Ron, smoker

However, some of the young men who obtained
apprenticeships were dissatisfied because it did not live up to
their expectations. Rather than variety and excitement they
found that their job was very tedious. For example, Frank, a
trainee technician:

> "It's been disappointing (...) It's not what I expected
> (....) It's too repetitive. All the jobs we do the same
> thing, day in, day out"
>
> Frank, smoker

However, it was the unskilled or semi-skilled jobs which
were the most boring. This was especially so for those young men
who had aimed at acquiring a trade. For example, Guy who had
hoped to become a chef got a job as a semi-skilled worker in a
brandy-snap biscuit factory. Instead of a step on the ladder to
a career this job provided little training and little
prospects for the future. Jim thought he was lucky when he
obtained a job as an apprentice upholsterer after leaving
school. Six months later his hopes of completing his
apprenticeship were dashed when the factory closed.
Subsequently he found a job as a machine minder which he found
very boring:

> "There's just nothing right about the place (....)I
> don't like it but there's no place else to go to [I'd
> like] a decent job thats well-paid"
>
> Jim, non-smoker

In this atmosphere of boredom smoking can become valuable to
some young men. Rather than standing idle, the act of smoking can
give the young worker the illusion of doing something. As Frank
said:

45

"....if I'm bored and got nothing to do I like to sit
and have a fag and a think."
Frank, smoker

The ex-smokers and non-smokers seemed especially aware of the
routine work conditions which encouraged smoking. Derek,
an apprentice electrician, who had given up smoking remembered
when he would smoke at work:

"I'd have one in the vans travelling a lot, y'know. I
do a lot of travelling (....) It gets boring"
Derek, ex-smoker

Several of the people Jim worked with smoked. Although he
himself did not smoke he could understand why some of them did:

"Cause they're bored. I think boredom causes most of it"
Jim, non-smoker

George who rarely smoked at work agreed:

"If I had a boring job I would, I think, but as I'm
interested in what I'm doing I don't smoke".
George, smoker

Few of the young women who had unskilled jobs described their
work in much detail. It was usually extremely tedious repetitive
work. Sarah, a housewife, recalled her job:

"All I used to do was stick these (...) little diamonds
on jumpers."
Sarah, smoker

Smoking was not uncommon among these young women. To smoke was
to do something which was personally satisfying unlike the
tedium of routine work.

The young women who had obtained non-manual work often
expressed more intrinsic satisfaction, especially if the job
offered variety and responsibility. Linda, a clerk, initially
felt frustrated at the repetitive nature of her work but this had
changed:

"I've taken on further responsibilities now so I'm
alright at the moment."
Linda, non-smoker

Without such responsibility office work could be as boring as
factory work. Vicki also worked as a clerk but found:

"I just get through the day, y'know, think: 'Oh, I'm
going out tonight, where am I going?"
Vicki, smoker

While Christine who had recently given up her job in an
office remembered:

"When I was at school I always wanted to work in an

office (....) I hated it though because it was the same thing, day in, day out".

Christine, smoker

Fortunately, Christine subsequently managed to find a more interesting job as a nurse about which she said:

"I wouldn't want to change it now. I couldn't go back to the other thing."

Christine, smoker

Without some degree of variety and responsibility the risk of smoking seemed to grow. Tracey was a nursery nurse. She was extremely happy with her work:

"I enjoy my job very much (....) I enjoy going to work. I think it must be awful for somebody who hates to go to work"

Tracey, smoker

Although Tracey smoked, she rarely did so at work.

4.5 Breaks

Most of the workers' daily routine was broken up by both official and unofficial breaks. These were an important part of their workday. They not only provided a release from the actual work but also an opportunity for socializing with workmates. Dennis described his break system:

"I'm supposed to start at half past seven but I usually get there about eight o'clock (....) We have an unofficial tea break - twenty past eight till about twenty five to nine - have a cup of tea and that. We have an official break at ten o'clock and then a dinner break (....) and then we have another break at three o'clock till ten past and we finish at half past four"

Dennis, smoker

These breaks usually involved leaving the immediate workplace and going to the canteen or a rest room. For example:

"We've got our own little room - sit there and have dinner, cuppa tea and that with me mates 'cause I don't see them sort of during the day so much"

Frank, smoker

Part and parcel of these breaks for the manual workers was often a cigarette. Again Dennis:

"Everybody, y'know, lights a fag, y'know, at breaktimes. Its, you have a fag, I'll have one. You have a cup of tea and your breakfast and then you wont have a fag all morning afterwards. Its like a dessert pudding. Oh, I'll have a fag, yeah".

Dennis, smoker

Or as George, the upholsterer put it:

> "It's always, y'know, when you have a cup of coffee,
> have a fag"
>
> George, smoker

Smoking was sometimes integrated into their work routine by these workers. Dennis described this well:

> "I have one while I'm working (.....) You're allowed to
> smoke y'know (....) I get through about twenty a day
> (...) If I'm really busy time flies without me really
> noticing it and I don't have time for a fag but (....)
> usually this job you're doing on a bus you'll get
> working on it and then you've got to wait for like the
> paint to dry a bit or while you're working something out
> you've sort of just convenient timed it right, no matter
> what you're doing to have a fag. It just, it just works
> right.... Sometimes if you're rushed time flies and you
> don't realise and you think: 'Oh, I haven't had many
> fags today'"
>
> Dennis, smoker

Smoking was not just a part of Dennis's work routine but a valuable aid to the regulation of time for particular jobs.

However, where there were restrictions on smoking this use of smoking was not apparent. For example, George, the apprentice upholsterer, described how having to leave the factory floor for a smoke could disrupt the work routine rather than assisting in its regulation:

> "In the afternoon you can go for a fag if you like but I
> don't smoke at work now (....) You can't smoke in the
> shop-floor so it means stopping and starting all the
> time (....) I used to when I first started but you just
> get into a rhythm of doing something and then you go for
> a fag and you lose it"
>
> George, smoker

Similarly, Bill the engineer found that the effort involved in having a smoke disrupted his work routine too much rather than helping in it's regulation:

> "The only time I really smoke is dinner times and breaks
> because I work with oil and I have oil all over my hands
> so I never smoke when I've got oil all over me hands.
> Like a lot of lads will go to the toilet and wash it. If
> I'm not busy I'll go down and wash me hands and have a
> fag but its mainly just dinner times and breaks and
> thats it"
>
> Bill, smoker

But for many manual workers to have a cigarette meant to have a break and conversely to not have a cigarette meant to not have a break. Barry, a student who had a temporary holiday job in a factory, recalled that the workers there used smoking as a means to a break:

"I'm working at the moment at the pop factory near here. Everybody smokes, y'know, everybody. Apart from me, virtually, all the workers, they all smoke (...) I mean, for one thing, they can have five minutes off if they want to have a fag say, so its a break"

Barry, non-smoker

For the young women who worked in the factories the breaks, both official and unofficial, were very important for regulating the day. Marion, a machinist, described the importance of cigarettes in creating breaks:

"You're supposed to have one in the morning and you can have one at break-one in the afternoon and one at break and then one at dinner. But I go for one before break, one after break and, one in the afternoon and then one at break in the afternoon"

Marion, smoker

In some places there were few official breaks but to stop for a cigarette enabled an unofficial break for these young women from their boring and monotonous work. Hilary described this:

"There's no breaks there. You get half an hour dinner time but you don't get a break in the day. But you can smoke and drink, you can take a wander round if you like. They don't say anything."

Hilary, smoker

However, in some workplaces, having a break on the shop floor was not accepted by management - the constant monotonous work had to be maintained. In this situation the young women often escaped to the only place out of sight of management - the toilet. Here they were unlikely to be disturbed and could have a cigarette in comfort. Sarah, one of the young mothers, remembered this well:

"We would say we were going to the toilet and have a quick cigarette (....) As long as they didn't catch you. If they caught you, well, you'd be in trouble, sort of thing. But it was alright. We used to always go in about every hour, something like that"

Sarah, smoker

Jenny, who did not smoke, noticed her fellow workers taking these unofficial smoking breaks:

"They'll clear off - start at about half seven, and half eight they'll go for one. Then they'll go for break at quarter past nine and come back again. Then they go for one about half eleven (....) They go downstairs in toilet - out the way"

Jenny, non-smoker

Various techniques had been developed by management to control these unofficial breaks. The most popular method was the use of piecework which provided financial reward for those workers who worked consistently. Some workers liked it:

"Ours is a piecework job and I'm on the go all the time

49

> "(....) I enjoy it.... don't get bored, keeps you on the
> go all the time"
>
> Jenny, non-smoker

For these workers a break for a cigarette incurred a
financial penalty and so they were less likely to take many
breaks.

4.6 Social relations at work

One of the most valued attributes of work was the social
relations with fellow workers. Indeed, many workers judged the
quality of their work-life by the quality of their social life
there. Again, there were many interesting sex and social class
differences in the character of social relations at work. For the
male manual workers, there was little contact with women at work.
Bill, an apprentice engineer, described his friends at work:

> "There's like a row of blokes, y'know, and we all have a
> good laugh, fantastic (....) They're a great bunch of
> kids"
>
> Bill, smoker

Similarly, Brian another apprectice engineer:

> "[I work with] a bunch of lads. Well, I'm in a workshop.
> There's about thirty in the workshop. On our section
> about five of us, good mates"
>
> Brian, smoker

It would seem that smoking formed an important aspect of these
young men's social interaction at work. Dennis, the
coachbuilder, described the role of smoking:

> "Y'know , you offer them round and they offer them back
> and that (....) There's about half of us on our
> particular gang [who smoke] but the majority of lads at
> our garage smoke"
>
> Dennis, smoker

However, some young males did not have much
opportunity for interaction at work because of the nature of
their jobs. Ken, the young painter, spent most of his time:

> "With the radio, mainly (....) A lot of the time you're
> sort of split up on a building site."
>
> Ken, non-smoker

Similarly Terry, the sheet-metal worker, often found himself
alone at work:

> "You're actually independent (...) unless you go out
> on a job (....) but otherwise you work on your own"
>
> Terry, non-smoker

These more individual workers were often non-smokers. In
their work situation the social value of smoking was low.

The intensity of social interaction was also related to smoking at work. Many male manual workers did not smoke although they often worked as a group. However, although they participated in the group workwise, some of these young men seemed reluctant to develop further the social bonds with their fellow workers. For example, Tim, the apprentice engineer, mentioned working with a group:

> "There's about twenty employees. Its not a very big place, you know everybody. You work sort of... you're not on your own, you work as a team, y'know, don't feel as if you're on your own"
>
> Tim, non-smoker

However, Tim's abiding interest was running and during his lunch break, his main opportunity for developing closer social relations, he went out jogging alone:

> "There's no breaks or anything. There's only three quarters of an hour dinner and I'm not in the factory. I go out and run"
>
> Tim, non-smoker

Similarly, Jim, who worked with a group of three other men minding various textile machines did not smoke although the others did. Jim, a young West Indian, did not identify with his workmates, two of whom were middle-aged men who he considered unhealthy. His aim was to become a skilled worker whereas they seemed resigned to their lot:

> "They just stand about smoking but they're working at the same time. They don't actually stop to have a fag (....) They just smoke all the time (....) They've got filthy habits"
>
> Jim, non-smoker

For the young women who had unskilled factory jobs the most important aspect of their work was their friendships. Several emphasised that it was more important than wages. Hilary, a machinist, had changed jobs several times but was content in her present position:

> "It's crap money but I like the job, I like the girls.... I think if you like a job thats the most important thing - if you get on alright there"
>
> Hilary, smoker

Although Hilary was denied the opportunity of obtaining an interesting job with good wages at least she could have good work mates. Similarly Marion, who had tried working in a small office for a while, returned to factory life because of her friends, despite lower wages:

> "I really missed them when I left because I was working with [only] three people in the city. I was working in a really big factory in Peakside."
>
> Marion, smoker

Valerie had stopped work since marrying and having a

baby. Her fondest memories of her unskilled factory job were her
friendships:

> "I never had to think on that job, it was the same every
> day but it was a nice factory with a nice atmosphere"
>
> Valerie, smoker

For these young women smoking was an important facet of
their all-female social relations at work. It seemed to help
build social bonds with workmates and in doing so reduced the
intolerable nature of the monotonous routine of their work.
The sharing of cigarettes reinforced human relations in the
rather inhuman factory atmosphere. A whole ritual of sharing
cigarettes developed between these young women. Sometimes the
nature of this ritual seemed to become a means of quantifying the
extent of friendship between workmates. Hilary, a young
machinist, described such:

> "Patricia, the girl who sits in front of me, she's never
> got no money and she's never got no fags but if she's
> got one cigarette she'd give it to you, so we all just
> hand them round. Like the last fortnight I said no, I'm
> not putting them round anymore, we'll all smoke our own
> because, y'know, I'm giving out all my fags (....) more
> than I've smoked because some smoke more than others
> (....) But I still give one to Pat because she's never
> got any. But we try and keep it to ourselves as much as
> we can now"
>
> Hilary, smoker

One factory, realising the importance of smoking in aiding
social interaction had provided a table which became known as
the 'smoking table' where the women could sit for a while and
smoke as a break from the work routine. The 'smoking table' was
actually on the factory floor and became a focus for social
interaction.

Emma, who was a semi-skilled factory worker, enjoyed little
social life at work. The reason for this was that she did not
work on the factory floor with the majority of the women. Instead
she worked with a small group of older women with whom she had
little in common. The social bonds between them were slight. In
this situation the value of smoking at work was slight to Emma:

> "I've never smoked at work. Occasionally if I feel like
> one I'll go out and have one but not very often"
>
> Emma, smoker

In many ways her work situation was like that of Jim,
described earlier, who preferred to limit his social relations
with his workmates.

The non-manual male workers did not have extensive social
relations at work. Sometimes their position of responsibility
removed them from regular social interaction with their
workmates. Graham, the trainee manager, tended to consider the
other shop workers inferior. Although his wages were lower, his
position had status. He rarely mixed with the other workers.

Len worked in the family business. His fellow workers were two young women. Whereas their future was probably marriage and, if lucky, a return to a similar work position, Len planned on becoming a manager. His family connections and his future work plans tended to remove him from equitable social relations with the two women.

Not surprisingly, neither Graham nor Len smoked. Their social relations at work provided little incentive to smoke.

The young women who gained non-manual jobs often did not have extensive social relations at work. Although most seemed content with their job, there was less the collective identity expressed by those in manual jobs. The character of office work not only meant that there was less opportunity for co-operation between workers but the individual relationship with superiors often restricted the development of any feeling of solidarity with colleagues. While conflicts in the factory were usually in the terms of 'the boss and us' in the office it was often in terms of 'the management and me'.

In the office there seemed to be fewer set breaks. Coffee was often drunk at the desk thus restricting further the opportunity for developing social bonds between workers. In this atmosphere the social value of smoking was much reduced.

Often in the offices, unlike in the factories, there were restrictions on smoking. Susan who worked in a large typing pool described these:

> "You're not supposed to walk around carrying one around. You can sit down and smoke at your desk and have one but you're not supposed to walk around with one"
>
> Susan, non-smoker

By separating smoking from social interaction such restrictions reduced further the social value of smoking.

However, sometimes these restrictions could be counter-productive. One young woman reported on the segregation of smokers from non-smokers in her office:

> "We've got eight desks in the room divided into two halves, four in each, and the smokers sit one end and the non-smokers sit the other"
>
> Vicki, smoker

These half restrictions may have actually increased the social value of smoking by forcing the smokers together where they had greater opportunity for sharing cigarettes as part of the process of building social bonds. The character of the work itself often prevented young non - manual workers from developing social relations. Tracey who had a job as a nursery nurse found she was in an intermediate position between the teaching and auxiliary staff in the school. This position tended to obviate against the development of comfortable social relations since she was not readily accepted by the teachers and she wanted to maintain her status with the other staff. Although Tracey smoked, she smoked little at work:

> "I suppose if I had a break in the morning, if I left
> and sat in the staff-room, then I would have a
> cigarette then. But as it is, I don't (...) only a
> few of us smoke, the majority don't (...) We don't
> tend to smoke together".
>
> Tracey, smoker

Without the equitable social relations the social value of
smoking was reduced.

4.7 Image of the worker

Most of the young apprentices readily identified with
their particular trade. They were proud to be acquiring
skills and were eager to give details of their job. Dennis,
the apprentice coach-builder, was particularly scathing about
work-mates who were less skilled than himself:

> "Now he's come onto our gang he thinks he's a fully
> skilled coachbuilder and he's just an absolutely useless
> labourer like (...) I told the gaffer I don't want to
> work with him. So there's one of the fully skilled
> blokes (....) I work with him or I work on my own"
>
> Dennis, smoker

The identification with the manual/masculine aspect of the job
was apparent in his later commments:

> "I wouldn't like a job sitting down pen-pushing. (....)
> I prefer rolling in the mud like, getting on with it,
> using me hands"
>
> Dennis, smoker

He was quite proud of his strength:

> "I can do a days work without feeling tired"
>
> Dennis, smoker

A strong man like him could handle cigarettes:

> "I never smoked at school because as a kid it can
> cripple you at an early age but like if you give it a
> chance for your body to mature so it can cope with it a
> bit better it's not so bad"
>
> Dennis, smoker

Concern with status and image was very important to many of the
young women who worked in offices. Great importance was attached
to dress, manner and presentation. Part and parcel of some of
the jobs seemed to be the ability to project a good image of the
firm. For example, Katherine the bank clerk described this:

> "I think its a bit pressurised because you're in contact
> with people most of the time as a cashier and you've got
> to be polite no matter what mood you're in. You've got
> to be nice to the customer"
>
> Katherine, non-smoker

The importance of the correct image would conflict with any desire to smoke in this sort of job. This was apparent in another comment by Katherine:

> "There's very few people who do smoke as they're aware that we don't like it (....) Our manager doesn't like customers to see them and I think they respect people who don't smoke, as well"
>
> Katherine, non-smoker

This concern with presenting a 'good' image was not something which perturbed the young women in the factory.

4.8 Stress at work

Few workers mentioned stress when describing their work routine. Such components of stress as heavy workload and responsibility, time urgency, etc, were not mentioned at all. Despite this several non-smokers thought that stress at work might encourage smoking. Katherine the bank clerk, described the situation when some of her colleagues smoked:

> "Sometimes you get a crisis on your hand (....) and you hear the occasional person say 'Oh, I must have a cigarette'. So I think thats one of the times when they do have to smoke really - they get a bit under pressure or something".
>
> Katherine, non-smoker

Penny who had given up smoking and had lost her job remembered:

> "When I was at work I smoked because I was under pressure and it sort of calmed my nerves a bit."
>
> Penny, non-smoker

A few smokers agreed that stress at work might encourage smoking. Peter, the shop assistant, smoked:

> "When things aren't going right, its as simple as that".
>
> Peter, smoker

While Hilary, the machinist, smoked:

> "If you have rows, and when you have, you just light a cigarette up instead of shouting at her [supervisor]"
>
> Hilary, smoker

Of course many of the young people who reported stress at work did not smoke. Guy, the trainee cook, frequently had problems with his boss such that after work he felt:

> "Tired...the strain, not actually 'cause of work, just strain of the boss (....) anything goes wrong we all get done for it".
>
> Guy, non-smoker

Stress, per se, was not sufficient for smoking but some of the
young people had learned to use smoking as a means of coping with
stress.

4.9 Future plans

Many of the young men who were finishing their
apprenticeships were planning progress to a better job. Indeed
it could be said that by becoming a fully skilled tradesman such
planning became possible. Ken who was just finishing his
apprenticeship as a painter was considering going independent:

> "I'd like to, probably, in a couple of years, set up on
> my own".

Ken, non-smoker

Some of these young men were considering moving from manual
to non-manual work. However, such mobility was difficult to
achieve and required a fierce determination besides the
provision of opportunities. Tom, an apprentice upholsterer,
described the division between office staff and the shop floor
worker and the difficulties involved in crossing this divide:

> "In a way I wish I'd have stayed on in school, sixth
> form ...but in another way I'm glad I left when I
> did ... people since have found it hard to get jobs
> straight away whereas I had lots of choices...I could
> have had a better job like (...) 'cause I'd be on
> staff...It's like at work...it's like that staff are
> above the workers.. they've got something over
> us...'slike this youth who stayed on at sixth form he
> went straight into wages (....) It's like he's got
> authority over me (....) Yet I was in a higher class
> than him in school. Just 'cause he stayed on in school.
> But in the long run I can if I'm going to college and
> get all me City and Guilds I might be able to get
> another job.... He's like....had to be without money.
> Perhaps he had pocket money as a part-time job
> while he was in school, but he didn't have a wage coming
> in since school(....) I've been at college,
> like,....and he comes out and gets better money than
> me.... or he was. Now I'm qualified I'm better than him"

Tom, non-smoker

Tom was determined:

> "I could do one more year at college and pass (....)
> finals and then try and get on to a management course
> or.... teacher training college"

Tom, non-smoker

The non-smokers seemed particularly concerned about their
future plans. However, some smokers also detailed plans for
their career. These tended to be young men who were frustrated
with their current position. Peter, after failing his exams, had
obtained a job in his friend's father's shop. He found the
routine chores tedious and longed for something more interesting:

"But the boss is on about retiring and leaving it to his son, my friend(....) so eventually I hope to become a partner... that's if he does give it to his son".
Peter, smoker

Some of the young women who had managed to obtain office jobs were planning future progress. Again, these were mostly non-smokers. Helen had a clerical job in an office but had career ambitions and had taken steps to achieve them:

"I am taking college for further qualifications (...) to get qualifications (....) Because you don't get anywhere unless you're determined".
Helen, non-smoker

However, for these young women there was the conflict between career ambitions and the traditional attributes of the female role. For example, Katherine, the bank clerk:

"I don't want to go too high (....) I just want to be happy in my work (...) I don't want too much responsibility at work (...) I don't think its a woman's place to be career minded"
Katherine, non-smoker

In addition, cutting across career plans were marriage plans. For many young women work was, in reality, only temporary. As Mary put it:

"I intend to keep on working for a couple of years but I do want to get married, settle down and have a family"
Mary, non-smoker

The young women who worked in the factories had few ambitions as regards work. Their future plans were vague. There was little opportunity for promotion at work. At the moment most of them were enjoying the independence which having a wage gave. Although marriage would shortly curtail the work life of most of these young women it was not something seriously considered. Their concern was more with enjoying the present rather than planning for the future. Smoking was something they could enjoy now, health risks could be worried about later.

4.10 Motherhood

Five young women had married, had children and had given up full-time work. Marriage, in effect, for these women meant having children and looking after these children at least until they could attend school. During that period these women felt that the only suitable outside employment was part-time. Even then, child care could not be neglected:

"I've got a part-time job at the moment (....) I still have to take William with me. I feel as though once your a mum thats it....you've got to be a mum"
Debbie, non-smoker

Further, it was felt that a good mother must look after her own children:

> "I'd like to [get a job] but then I wouldn't dream of putting him in a nursery."
>
> Sally, non-smoker

Sometimes, the husband discouraged thoughts of a return to work outside the home:

> "I don't think he'd like me to go back to work to start with (...) 'cause he still doesn't really want me to do what I want"
>
> Sally, non-smoker

The non-smokers seemed more prepared to accept this role. The smokers seemed frustrated. They longed to return to the social interaction which work provided.

The young women attempted to bring some structure into their home life routine. It usually involved housework, child care, shopping and various other tasks interspersed with breaks which sometimes involved social contact with other young mothers. Debbie described a typical day:

> "Mm, clean from top to bottom. Usually I'm done by twelve, if I'm doing upstairs. Then I sit and watch tele with William (....) asleep, so I decide to wash the baby's clothes, y'know. Do the babys clothes that I put away or just general cleaning, dusting again, just to keep myself occupied, or round about two o'clock if he's awake we'll go out and meet his dad if he's on mornings and then if we've got to go to the shops we'll go to the shop and then come back again, but evenings I don't go out"
>
> Debbie, non-smoker

Some young women were particularly frustrated by this routine and actively sought social contact with friends or relatives outside the home. As Jill said:

> "If you sat in all day it wouldn't be worth doing anything, would it? It's sort of boredom. Same thing every day"
>
> Jill, non-smoker

For those young women who smoked, social contact provided an opportunity for smoking. Valerie went out quite often to see friends. She always smoked with them.

Sarah, who smoked, spent most of her day at home with her unemployed husband. Both of them smoked primarily because of the boredom of homelife and the stress of child care. As Sarah, said:

> "I smoke the most at night time. Well all the rest of the day I'm that busy cleaning up and that like, it don't really bother me but at night time I've got

> nothing to do - thats when I sit down and smoke like a chimney - don't I?"
>
> Sarah, smoker

While her husband Carl added:

> "I mean, if the money wasn't so short as what it is I think probably (...) we'd smoke more 'cause, as I say, we're both at home. Neither of us is working and during parts of the day you get that fed up and miserable because he's [baby] awake nearly all night"
>
> Carl, smoker

For many young mothers smoking was perceived as a valuable aid to organizing their everyday routine which was bereft of the fixed schedule enjoyed by those in full-time employment.

4.11 Student life

Five young people, all from middle class homes, had gone to University. All but one of them were non-smokers and she, as explained earlier, had started smoking when she had a temporary job in a factory. Another girl had also worked with smokers in a factory but unlike Alison she did not mix with them and did not adopt smoking. She recalled her former workmates:

> "Most people I met did smoke (....) They weren't allowed to smoke during working hours. They were allowed to smoke at lunch and at breaks. At lunch- time I would tend to go and sit outside because it was baking hot but during breaktime I'd go and sit with them"
>
> Judith, non-smoker

After the initial enthusiasm of gaining entry to college the students work life fell into a routine which some of them found boring. For example, Judith:

> "Actually I find it rather boring because we only have eleven hours of lectures a week and I tend to sleep in the afternoons. Sounds dreadful but its true"
>
> Judith, non-smoker

With such a small proportion of their worklife formally organized the student had to learn how to organize the remainder him or herself. There were certain similarities with the unorganized day of the unemployed and young mothers.

Matthew suggested that when his fellow students had work to do then they were unlikely to smoke:

> "I suppose in some ways its because they're occupied doing something else. In areas like the library and lectures, I mean, they're already occupied"
>
> Matthew, non-smoker

But as with other workers the prime time for students to smoke was in their breaktimes. Judith noted this:

"They are allowed to smoke during lectures if they want to and there's one or two of them that do, including some lecturers, but most of the time it's on our breaktime or dinnertime".

Judith, non-smoker

Roger went further:

"In between long, boring lectures when we have a fifteen minute break, its quite common, in the common room, all pile down to the common room to get drinks, criticise the lecturer"

Roger, non-smoker

The problem of organizing the unstructured time outside the lectures seemed to be especially acute for the students with fewest formal classes. Alison studied English and found she had a "lot of free time" which was often spent socialising. It was in these extended breaks that smoking was popular.

4.12 Life in the armed forces

Three young men had joined the forces after leaving school. Several others had applied but had failed to gain acceptance for various reasons. Indeed among working class boys life in the forces seemed to offer a very attractive future of excitement and security. One of the young men had recently left the army. The other two were keen to remain. They had always intended a life in the forces. Sam joined the army:

"I always wanted to do it. I was pretty sure when I left school I was going to get it (...) I wouldn't swop. I wouldn't swop for anything.[The future] holds a lot actually (....) I've stacks more City and Guilds qualifications to get if I stay in (....) The longer you do the more qualifications you get (....) and there's promotion as well. They all mean more money."

Sam, smoker

Mick joined the navy:

"I wanted to join the navy (....) There no particular reason for it (...) I hope to stay for the next two and a half years....then a job for twelve years after that (....) I'll probably sign up for another [12 years] because the money never fluctuates (...) and it's a secure job if you don't make a mess up and you're good at your job they'll take you for twelve years"

Mick, non-smoker

The ex-soldier, however, was glad to leave the army. The discipline was the aspect which he found most irksome:

"I liked Germany but not the army, like (....) I got on alright with most of them. It was the officers I didn't get on with very well"

John, smoker

In many respects the career of Sam and Mick mirrored those of the social and unsocial manual worker. Sam did not smoke before joining the army. Then the adult norm and the social camaraderie of life in the army combined to encourage him to start:

> "I went to the Army Selection centres where they decide whether you are good enough for the army, y'know. You decide what trade you want to do (....) I had me first cigarette there, I think it was and it just progressed from there"
>
> Sam, smoker

Social bonds between the young soldier were very strong. The importance of smoking in maintaining these social bonds was apparent in Sam's comments:

> "I never used to smoke when I was at school (...) I used to have the odd drag (...) just out of curiosity like (...) I think I started smoking when I joined the forces (....) A lot of lads do, y'know. You get lots who have never even tasted a cigarette before they go in. You get a room full of lads and they're all smoking and passing them round and eventually you pick the habit up, y'know, and if you don't smoke you got all the smoke anyway coming in."
>
> Sam, smoker

Conversely, Mick considered the social life in the Navy to be fraught with tension due to the over-closeness of continued social contact with the same people:

> "There's a class of ten of us at the moment and we spend most of the time with just that ten (...) you don't get to know people very well (...) When you get a group of blokes together its natural that you're gonna get somebody taking it out on another."
>
> Mick, ex-smoker

Mick used to smoke but unlike Sam he often smoked on his own and not as part of social interaction:

> "When I did smoke I'd find it before exams in a stress situation or... once you get up in the morning.... classic one (...) at dinner time, y'know. Most people relax or go to sleep on the bed for an hour or so... thats when I found I used to smoke quite a bit or in class when you were bored"
>
> Mick, ex-smoker

Sam rarely smoked before ten o'clock in the morning. At work he was not allowed to smoke in the kitchens where he was a trainee chef but in his breaks he always smoked with the other young chefs:

> "You can't stop work for a cigarette in the kitchens (...) The only place you can smoke is in the rest room so the only chance you get when you are at work is at the NAAFI break at ten o'clock or during the lunch hour

> when you're finished for an hour (...) I usually have
> morning, lunch break, in the afternoon"
>
> Sam, smoker

To Sam, smoking was valued as a means of building comradeship with other young recruits. To Mick, reluctance to become involved with his mates reduced the value of smoking.

4.13 The unemployed

Six of the young people were currently unemployed. All had had different experiences of work and had been unemployed for varying lengths of time. Four of them, all young men, smoked. Indeed, for them smoking played a very important role in regulating their day. After the initial burst of searching for a job most now spent most of the day at home, doing nothing. When asked what he did during the day Rob replied:

> "Nothing much, just sit here all day"
>
> Rob, smoker

While Jason said:

> "In the day I just sit around the house or if I've got, y'know, some bus fare, I'll pop into Peakside."
>
> Jason, smoker

Often alone at home with nothing to do the main value of smoking was to disrupt the boredom. As Nick said:

> "Its 'cause I'm bored"
>
> Nick, smoker

Smoking seemed to be of value to these young men as a means of regulating the time. This was apparent in Jason's comment on the effect and use of tipped and rolled cigarettes:

> "When I was smoking [tipped cigarettes I had] one an hour, really. I used to limit myself to one an hour. With these I just have one when I feel like it. Sometimes it can go on for hours on end, four hours, y'know."
>
> Jason, smoker

John had found another means of circumventing the expense of smoking cigarettes - he smoked cigars:

> "You don't need so many as what you do cigarettes like and its cheaper to smoke them than cigarettes"
>
> John, smoker

The reason for this was that he did not smoke a whole cigar in one go but rather he smoked it for a while then let it go out and smoked it again later. John had previously given up smoking but had started again on becoming unemployed:

> "Its just through boredom I started again"
>
> John, smoker

Other factors may be of importance in explaining smoking among the unemployed but boredom and time regulation were of special importance.

4.14 Summary

The comments by the young workers have revealed quite graphically that smoking has a valuable meaning within the context of work. On entry to work the adoption of smoking can be considered a symbolic part of the transition to adult life, in boring jobs it provides a means of separating oneself from the tedious work routine or from fellow workers who may identify with that kind of work; in relations with workmates it assumes an important value in regulating social interaction. In addition, those young workers whose jobs offered few prospects of promotion were more concerned about enjoying life as it was. They would be less concerned about distant problems such as the risk to their health of continued smoking.

The comments also illustrated the attempts by the young adults to articulate and give substance to their "earlier fantasies" (Levinson, 1978). Many of them were finding this incrasingly difficult because of the limited job opportunities. The consequent frustration was particularly apparent among the young women some of whom seemed to smoke as a means of coping with this frustration.

This chapter also considered the typical day of those who did not have a full-time job outside the home - mothers, unemployed and students. One characteristic of their day which tended to unite these different groups was the lack of an imposed structure. Jahoda (1982) has emphasized that one of the most deleterious consequences of unemployment is "the destruction of a habitual time structure for the working day". Admittedly, mothers have a certain structure imposed by the requirements of housework and of childcare and so too do the students by their timetable of lectures and course assignments. However, they too reported periods when time seemed to drag. Smoking seemed to be of value to some of these young people as a means of imposing structure on these periods.

5 Smoking at leisure

5.1 Introduction

Besides the particular tasks of the period of early adult transition Levinson (1978) also identified certain tasks which were common to the whole of the novice period. The four most important tasks were:

1) forming a Dream and giving it a place in the life structure;
2) forming mentor relationships;
3) forming an occupation;
4) forming love relationships, marriage and family.

In many respects the themes discussed in the previous two chapters were concerned with the young adults attempts to accomplish the first two tasks. They were concerned with how the young adults developed "a vague sense of self-in-adult-world" which they tried to give "greater definition" as they broke away from the adolescent self in the family and began to form an occupation and a mentoring relationship which is often "situated in a work setting".

The fourth task of forming love relationships can be considered as being intermeshed within the wider task of forming peer relationships in general. The young adults' attempts to accomplish these tasks were most apparent in their discussion of their leisure time.

The recreational activities of the young adults were the most important aspect of their day-to-day lives. Most spent the biggest part of their leisure time in the company of both sexes from the same age group. The men were also involved in many single-sex activities. The women were often dependent on men for their social activities. Although they spent time in single-sex company, it was less common than it was for the men. This was not true for those young married women with no job outside the home whose minimal social contact was nearly always with other women in similar situations.

The range of activities engaged in varied from the informal, unstructured activities such as hanging out in the market place, to the more formal, structured activities such as organized sports and night classes. Further details of the activities are provided in the following sections.

5.2 The pub

The pub was a very important focus for these young people's social life. Most of the men spent a large proportion of their leisure time in the pub in male company. The pattern was similar for manual and non-manual workers:

> "I go out quite a lot to a pub(....) I go with me mates
> (....) I just drink in the pub. In the summer I like
> sitting outside. [I go out] about 2 or 3 times [a week]
> I suppose."
>
> > Derek, ex-smoker

> "[I go to] nightclubs, discos, pubs, winebars"
>
> > Brian, smoker

The smokers were especially involved in this active social life which tended to be unstructured and informal. In such an atmosphere the exchange and sharing of cigarettes could help initiate, maintain and strengthen social bonds in the informal group. 'Crashing' cigarettes - the local term for sharing - was normal behaviour. Those smokers not participating were frowned upon:

> "[I smoke when out] only basically when somebody else
> has one. Say we're all out in a group, say, and we're
> all crashing the fags and that. Say if its somebody
> else's turn, I'd wait for them to get one out. I
> wouldn't light one of my own, I'd wait for him to get
> his out and if its my turn, I just wait about 10 minutes
> and get mine out (....) I can't handle that, people who
> just smoke their own. It don't seem right."
>
> > Brian, smoker

The young men who did not smoke also frequented the pubs. Several of them were involved in specific activities there:

> "I sometimes play darts, not as often as I used to, but
> I sometimes play cards, depends on where we go."
>
> > Ken, non-smoker

> "Wednesdays and Thursdays I play pool."
>
> > Graham, non-smoker

The establishment of strong social bonds may be less important in such situations. In fact, Graham, an enthusiastic snooker player, was reluctant to develop strong relations with other players:

> "I don't get into people's lives fully like that. I just

65

know them as friends of the pool team or friends of the karate club and that's it."

Graham, non-smoker

If exchanging and sharing cigarettes was a sign of increasing intimacy it was not appealing to Graham who preferred to keep his distance.

When the young men went to the pub with their girlfriends, the event took on a different character. Sam, the young soldier, often drank with a group of soldiers when in the army. However, when home on leave, it was often just him and his girlfriend:

> "Sometimes we go to the disco (....) but she's quite content to just go out and have a quiet drink. She's not one for the rowdy night life, y'know (....) I'd just rather go an have a couple of beers, y'know. Have a game of pool with her and that. Make her happy, so I don't mind."

Sam, smoker

Sam's smoking behaviour changed with the change in the character of his social activities. When with his mates he smoked a lot:

> "The times I enjoy a cigarette most is when I'm out for a drink (....) When I go out for a drink I'll smoke more, y'know, more than I do otherwise during the day."

However, when he was with his girlfriend he rarely smoked:

> "[My girlfriend] pulls my leg (...) Fag-ash Lil she calls me, but I don't usually smoke when she's around. She don't like it (....) so I don't usually smoke when I'm with her."

The difference in the use of the pub by Sam in the army and Mick in the navy is useful in considering the recreational context within which smoking occurs. The lives of these young men as part of a close-knit male group in the forces was similar superficially. However, there were certain differences which could explain their different smoking practices. Sam talked of the strong social group with which he had become involved:

> "We all pile down on the football pitch, have a game of football amongst ourselves 'til about 8 o'clock, have a shower and a change. Some'll stay in and watch tele, some'll go down town, some'll go to the local pub across the road (...) nine times out of ten I'll go across the road for a few jars."

Sam, smoker

However, Mick tended to limit social contact when on leave:

> "If I go ashore, I usually go ashore with a couple of blokes and have a quiet drink somewhere, a talk.If not, I go ashore on me own and do me own thing."

Mick, ex-smoker

Sam became part of a social group in the army. He talked of how smoking was the norm within such a group and how he became a smoker on joining the army. He continued to smoke even though he was an avid sportsman and although he talked of limiting his smoking because of his sporting activities, he was not willing to give it up completely. Mick was not part of a social group where smoking was the norm. There would have been no value in the social act of smoking for him and he had, in fact, given up.

When the women talked about the pub being the centre for recreational activity it was evident that they were often dependent on their boyfriends or a larger mixed group of friends for this entertainment. It was not always satisfactory, particularly, it seemed, for the non-smokers:

> "[We] go to pub. Sit down and have a chat. Life's alright. Gets a bit boring sometimes (...) Doing the same things all the time (...) we do them all, each day, week in, week out, we haven't changed around."
>
> Jenny, non-smoker

Some women were more socially active and took a more active role in the groups to which they belonged. They were nearly always smokers:

> "Any spare time I've got, I'm always at the pub (...) 'cause that's where all me friends are you see."
>
> Marion, smoker

Vicki was an active pub-goer. She had a large circle of different groups of friends, a close girlfriend and a boyfriend. Her activities with each group were distinct and so was her smoking behaviour:

> "I always go out. I never stop in. I play darts. I play pool. I go swimming. I go for a drink with me friend (...) Saturday I tend to keep for me mate. We go to ... its the best night of the week."
>
> Vicki, smoker

She also spoke of the different groups of people she spent time with in different pubs:

> "One lot are really heavy rock sort of thing (....) they go in the biggest dives they can find and they won't dream of going into a really smart pub and yet I happen to do both."

Also, with Vicki and her friends it was the norm to crash cigarettes. However, crashing was not consistent between groups:

> "One group does [crash] and one group doesn't (...)The ones I hang round with mainly, they all do, but there's another group (...) I think one out of the whole lot has got a job so they can have about 2 halves a night and so many cigarettes."

She often travelled to country pubs with her boyfriend. It was apparent that then she restricted her smoking:

"[I smoke] most of the time [socially] (....) When I'm with [my boyfriend] I don't smoke as much. And if we go somewhere way out say and we're travelling in the car, I don't smoke in the car."

Vicki accounted for this decrease in smoking by the absence of crashing:

"There isn't anybody crashing so I don't smoke, [don't] bother to get them out as much."

Vicki, smoker

Without a boyfriend or a group of friends, the young women were less likely to visit the pub. Katherine described her predicament:

"Most of my friends have got steady boyfriends and they're engaged (. . .) If I had someone to share an evening with, if I had my way, I'd stay in all the time".

She was less enthusiastic about pub-life:

[I] just stay in mainly and perhaps my friend will come around and have a chat or something, but I'm not a going out person really (...) perhaps I might go for a drink in the week (...) we go to pubs at the weekend."

Katherine, non-smoker

For many of the young people smoking was an accepted part of their relations with a group of people when in the pub. When in the pub with only a boy or girlfriend smoking was less common.

5.3 Bikes and cars

The economic independence gained since leaving school had allowed some young people to acquire motorbikes and cars. It was nearly always the men who had done this. This was partly due to their higher wages. In the case of bikes an important factor was also the 'macho' image associated with owning and riding a large and powerful machine.

Frank was someone whose life seemed to revolve around his bike. It was a central part of his recreational activities whether that meant visiting the pub or travelling further afield to specific functions:

"[I go to] various pubs, concerts, rock concerts, if there's anything going on. [I] prefer to travel."

Frank, smoker

His weekends at home were taken up with cleaning and repairing his bike:

"Saturday morning [I] get up, clean the bike, polish it, do any work that needs doing, small jobs (....) sometimes go out for a ride."

Frank, smoker

The image of the biker was very important. Frank talked of spending most of the previous weekend shopping for the right sort of leather trousers for his biking mate. He had recently had his long hair cut to shoulder length and talked of how, now that he was getting older, he was feeling under more pressure to conform, whereas when he was younger he was able to ignore criticism.

The bikers appeared to be 'risk-takers' who enjoyed the dangers associated with biking. Several of Frank's friends had been killed in accidents and Dennis had recently been involved in one himself:

> "Someone did a U-turn in front of me. Head butted, me helmet come off and me head butted a bollard. That's part of being a biker, good fun. Go around butting bollards regular."
>
> Dennis, smoker

This tough man, 'macho' image was emphasised by the style of clothes and hair of the biker. Smoking 'strong' cigarettes was part of that style.

Those who were part of a biking group seemed to be very socially active. Dennis talked of the life of the bikers:

> "I usually go down to market place where they park all the cars, me and me mates cause I used to have a bike, we're all bikers, we all meet up and talk."
>
> Dennis, smoker

and Frank described his need for social life:

> "I enjoy [my social life] most of the time. I get a bit depressed sometimes when I go out and there's nobody turned up (....) As long as I can go to concerts, have a drink occasionally, get on with people, things like that, I'll be quite happy."
>
> Frank, smoker

Some young men who were enthusiastic bike-owners were less involved in the social side of bike ownership as described by Frank. The bikes were used as a form of transport, e.g. Terry used his bike to travel to his girlfriend's home every evening as she lived about ten miles away, or, as in Tony's case, as part of a sporting activity:

> "I also go to Speedway as well. Just over the road and I ride for the local cycle speedway team."
>
> Tony, non-smoker

These young men were non-smokers.

Since ending his bike riding days, Dennis had taken to driving a car. He was very proud of his car and curtailed his drinking because of it:

> "I don't drink much 'cause I've got a car."
>
> Dennis, smoker

Dennis's informal weekend activities depended on his car. It
enabled him to get away from his dull, routine, daily activities:

> "Usually what we do Friday and Saturday nights late at
> night 'til about 6 in the morning, we go up the motorway
> in my car (...) to a nightclub or we just go up and
> down the motorway for a ride. We all chip in on petrol
> and we just go for long rides and then kip out in the
> car all weekend, sleeping bags, reclining seats, like
> kip out. Summat different you know, get away from the
> usual thing, going to bed, getting up and going to work
> and that."
>
> Dennis, smoker

Dennis smoked.

Again, other young men adopted a more functional attitude to
owning a car - it was for getting them to and from work or some
social event. It was not a source of excitement in itself for
the car owner and his friends. Matthew, a student, had been
given a car by his parents. He used it mostly to drive to and
from University. Len used his car to travel to social events but
this was quite controlled.

> "Normally there's one or two of us.[We go] within a
> radius of 10 miles. Only having a drink at various pubs
> around."
>
> Len, non-smoker

Neither of these young men smoked.

5.4 "Hanging out"

Some young men spent most of their leisure time in totally
unstructured social situations. Guy was a mod who described his
unorganised social life:

> "[In the evenings I] usually go on the park (...) I
> used to go up there but I don't go up there much now.
> Just hang around in a gang, just muck about."
>
> Guy, non-smoker

He was not completely happy with this:

> "I would [enjoy my social life] if there was somewhere
> to go night like, just boring, y'know, boring places.
> Boring round 'ere. Nowhere to go."

His group of mod friends were often involved in fights
which provided excitement:

> "Most of [my friends] are mods (....) we're always in
> fights, especially when we get a few more together"

but Guy was not completely a part of this:

> "If someone's starting trouble I'd walk off. I don't

want to stand around for trouble but I don't think, its y'know, worth it (....) I'm going [to Skeggy] this Bank Holiday, but I'm not going in mod gear."

Guy had made a conscious decision to become a mod, perhaps in an attempt to break out of what was an even more boring social life:

"I've got some mates who just live down the road like and they just turned into mod (...) I was starting to hang around with this lad who just lived down the road (....) I got to know him and I had some money (...) I had about 80-90 quid I think it was, we went round town looking for something....suits y'know, two-tone suits and that. Just to get into mod like."

Although Guy was one of a group of mods, they were all younger than him and it seemed that he was not completely integrated into the 'scene'. He often stayed at home in the evenings:

"....otherwise I stop in or go for a walk round town or something [I've got] my own stereo upstairs like [I] put a speaker in the bathroom to listen to music, just soak in the bath and that, just listening. Going away to the beat. It's crazy...crazy for the sixties."
Guy, non-smoker

Music was an important part of the style of being a mod and Guy was able to enjoy it on his own. Although he was part of a larger group, he seemed to prefer these times spent alone. Guy did not smoke.

Dennis was also a member of a large, informal group which hung around casually in the market place:

"I usually go down the market place where they park the cars, me and me mates cause I used to have a bike. We're all bikers, we all meet up and talk (...) We all stand, y'know, see what action's about. It's sort of our territory. We stand there,talk and that, we don't cause no aggro 'cause we get on with all the Police like. We're good mates."
Dennis, smoker

Some of their activities were deliberately boisterous so as to attract the attention of others. Dennis explained:

"We have more fun. Like piggy back fights and all sorts, owt daft, just to get people to laugh (....) We do owt to get like an audience, get everybody laughing, have some fun."

Unlike Guy, Dennis was a regular member of the group. He rarely stayed in:

"I go down [the] market place, meet my mates (....) I'm out every night. Nowhere special."

Also in contrast to Guy, Dennis smoked. Most of the other smokers described how they crashed cigarettes but this was

71

not part of Dennis's routine when 'hanging out'. He shared cigarettes at work but:

"Usually hide your fags [down on the corner] because they're all scroungers and they ain't got none."

He emphasised that you only share if others do:

"Some of them are [on the dole] but even when they've got fags, there's that many, there's about eight or nine of us smokers, so if you've got a packet of twenty fags, you crash them out and half your packet has gone. I mean, that's half a quid down the drain. So you usually smoke your own, or don't light one up for a long while or you go and hide and light one up, yeah, out of the way."

Dennis's group of friends seemed to be very tight-knit and met up every evening, often spending weekends together sleeping out in his car (See Section 4.3). In such a tight-knit group there seemed to be an acceptance not to share cigarettes if many of the members were unable to crash in turn. Nevertheless Dennis still commented:

"A fag's part of being sociable. I mean ... OK if [others] don't smoke, they miss out (...) it saves me fags, but..."

Dennis, smoker

The rules of smoking at leisure seem to be influenced by economic factors. While those young men with good wages could afford to drink regularly and to share their cigarettes freely, those with poor wages or no job at all chose instead to 'hang out' at a street corner and to be more cautious in sharing cigarettes despite realising their social value.

5.5 Sports

Many of the young people were involved in sporting activities which they pursued seriously on a regular basis. It was usually the young men who were involved, with only one young woman mentioning specific sports. Examples of the sporting activities engaged in by the non-smoking men are apparent in the following comments:

"I play football, y'know, every Sunday. We've got a good team."

Ken, non-smoker

"After work (....) I go straight to the gym [I do] weight training (....) do a bit of cycling (....) and the odd jog once a week."

Tim, non-smoker

"I play football for a couple of sides. I play cricket every Wednesday night. I go jogging everyday and occasionally I also play football about twice a week."

Matthew, non-smoker

Most of the young people involved in such sports did not smoke. The organised nature of the sporting activities developed strong social bonds between the participants. The social value of smoking was less relevant to them. In addition, the unhealthy aspect of smoking probably had more meaning to them since smoking could restrict their sporting performance. Sam was an active sportsman who smoked. He realised the problem:

"I don't smoke a lot. I smoke about 8 or 10 a day cause I'm a very keen sportsman you see, so I can't afford to smoke that much."

Sam, smoker

Other young men, usually smokers, talked about sporting activities in a more casual way. Sport seemed to be much more a part of their general social activity rather than an activity pursued for its own sake:

"I go swimming a lot down the quarries and that (....) I camp out regular and we go round at night-time chopping wood and we go canoeing and that."

Dennis, smoker

"[I play] cricket generally on Saturday and Sunday (....) go for a pint afterwards."

Brian, smoker

Since the interest of these young smokers in sport was of a more casual nature they would be less concerned with the ill-effects of smoking on their ability to be involved. Brian gave up a serious weight training programme because he had to give up smoking and drinking in order to follow it.

Interest in professional football teams was another example of time spent on sporting activities:

"[On weekends I] go to a football match. I support Derby."

Tony, non-smoker

"I sometimes go and see Forest (...) and I'm hoping to save a bit of me money (...) to buy a new season ticket."

Darren, non-smoker

It was the non-smokers who had this interest in attending football matches. Attending soccer matches is usually an informal social activity. This is possibly the case for some young people who see it as a major social event. However, the impression gained from these young men was that they were committed fans who attended matches for the game rather than for the occasion. None of them smoked.

5.6 Going steady

Those young people who experienced a varied and active social life usually did so until they became involved in a

73

serious relationship. As marriage plans materialized social activities were curtailed:

> "[I drink] only shandies. I used to [drink] before I met Sheila and that. I used to go with my mates and that, y' know. For three years when I first started work, I did drink, yeah. Used to go out probably seven days a week [with] me mates round here, or girls or whatever. [My life's changed a lot] since I've had a steady girlfriend (...) I think its done me good really 'cause before y'know, you used to go through one girl after another, y'know, not really getting anywhere."
>
> Terry, non-smoker

Since becoming a father Tom's recreational activities had been halted:

> "Well, I gotta steady girlfriend, just had a daughter about a few weeks ago so. We're engaged, we're getting married like, so I stay in most of the time (...) I used to go to the pub quite a bit but since....(....) we don't go out that much. I used to spend quite a lot of time in [the] pub."
>
> Tom, non-smoker

Some young men seemed very reluctant to get drawn into steady relationships and seemed to prefer the single life they enjoyed with their mates:

> "If you've got a regular girlfriend and that, you've got to think about her as well and that. And [you] sometimes slips and if you slips you get into trouble and get a bollocking and you're in the doghouse, and, sometimes wonder if its worth the hassle and things like that. So I'm better off single for a few years yet. Got a girlfriend, yeah, but we're not married yet."
>
> Dennis, smoker

and Nick:

> "She knows I'm going out with me mates and spending money 'cause I enjoy doing that better than going out with her and spending money."
>
> Nick, smoker

The smokers seemed to have a more active social life which they were content with and they found it more difficult to accept the quieter life which seemed the norm for couples.

A similar situation existed for some of the young women: they did not want to get involved. Vicki, who had a steady boyfriend, kept Saturday night free to go out with a girlfriend:

> "It's the best night of the week. I don't want him to ruin it."
>
> Vicki, smoker

Marion had ended a long-term relationship with her boyfriend when most of her friends were looking towards marriage. She had even used smoking as an aid to asserting her independence:

"I went out with this lad and he hated smoking (....) he kept nagging me, going on, so I packed it all up. Went out with him for two years (...) he kept saying "Oh pack it in, pack it in" and then I started up again before I finished with him (...) I thought, sod it, why should I bother about him, you know, its me, my life."

Marion, smoker

These young people who adopted a more carefree attitude to relationships seemed more likely to smoke. Perhaps, this attitude to relationship was part of a more general lack of concern about future-planning.

5.7 Marriage

Marriage had a marked effect on the recreational activities of these young adults. All but one of our married couples had moved away from their parents and most had at least one child. The increased financial obligations accompanying these new situations nearly always meant a curtailment of leisure activities. The married men talked about keeping in contact with friends and about how their friends now visited them in their homes. Unstructured, informal activities had changed their base from the pub to the home:

"I've got a few [mates] but not to say as I go out with them most nights (...) they come round and see me and what not (...) last time I went out was two weeks ago."

Ron, smoker

Some of these young men stressed the importance of maintaining their friendships. Bill had kept up his involvement in the local carnival band and Ron preferred by far the summer months activity in Bellstown where he had a seasonal job:

"There's a lot more activity and people up there and meeting different people. There's not the same old faces all the time and the same things happening in the pub. Everything's different up there you know."

Ron, smoker

Smoking for these young men had always been part of their social activity and Bill's wife saw it as a small luxury which Bill was allowed:

"We don't go out a lot drinking really (....) you can't stop everything can you (....) you can't give up everything just because you got married, can you?"

Bill's wife, non-smoker

For the women, married with young children and no job outside the home, it was more difficult to distinguish between worktime (houseworktime) and leisure time. When asked what they did in their free time they often replied "We don't go out much" implying that in order for an activity to be recreational it had to take place outside the home with their

75

husband. It was the smokers who appeared to be more socially active:

> "Well, we don't go out a lot, we haven't got enough money. We go out now and again (....) quite often in a group."
>
> Valerie, smoker

> "We usually go out round the corner to the pub."
>
> Sarah, smoker

Even without young family commitments the non-smokers were much less active socially:

> "Well, we haven't been out for quite a while. Sometimes we go to the old place but we don't really make a habit of say, going out every Friday night. But since we've been married we said we would, we'd go out a night each week, didn't we? But we haven't got round to it yet."
>
> Susan, non-smoker

These early years of marriage were not a time for developing new social relationships. Rather it was often a period in which the partners established a new life on their own. As such it did not provide the wider social contact in which smoking was valued unless the friendships established before marriage were maintained.

5.8 On the dole

The unemployed young people had coped with their status with varying degrees of success. The one unemployed young woman, Penny, who had previously been training to be a nurse, seemed less bothered about finding things to do in her extra time. This may have been due to her being used to the experience of shift work during her nurse training:

> "[I] have a mooch around the Job Centre. Sometimes I stop in like I have today and try and do some housework. Visit the library, this sort of thing."
>
> Penny, ex-smoker

Penny used to smoke only in the breaks at work and was a light smoker. The break-time opportunity for smoking did not present itself to her anymore and her social interaction was now minimal. These may have been the reasons for her having given up smoking. Penny had a boyfriend with whom she spent most evenings. He was employed and possibly helped to finance her recreational activities. She did not complain about having little money whereas the unemployed young men nearly always commented that their social activities were restricted for financial reasons. Most were in the position of having employed friends and this always caused problems, not only because of lack of money, but also because of a lack of understanding on the part of those employed:

> "Well me mates sort of say, "How long you been on the dole now?" and I say "about 6 months." [They] say

"blooming 'eck," y'know, "that's a long time." If they
went a month or week on the dole they'd realize how hard
it is. They can't see how hard it is for me. They say
"are you coming out?" and I say "I haven't got any
money," and they say, y'know, "come out anyway." They
can't see it, y'know, just bring out ten pound notes
every night 'cause they've all got jobs. I don't
think I've got a mate who hasn't got a job."

> Nick smoker

Nick only smoked when he was with his friends and it was
possible that he saw it as an activity which allowed him to
remain part of the group to which he belonged. He was able to
take part in the sharing of cigarettes which may have helped him
to keep his position in the group.

Because of lack of money the unemployed found that there was
little to do other than stay at home:

"[I do] nothing much really, just stay in."

> Nick, smoker

"[I do] nothing much. Just sit here all day."

> Rob, smoker

Visits to the Job Centre became less of an activity as the
length of unemployment increased. The futility of the exercise
quickly became apparent but it was still occasionally seen as
something to do:

"I used to go down town a lot. I used to go to the Job
Centre a lot. Just go every couple of weeks [now] and
sign on."

> John, smoker

Most of the unemployed were smokers. Lack of money meant they
had to reduce their consumption or stop smoking manufactured
cigarettes. Jason had done the latter:

"I've gone on to smoking roll-ups now 'cause its a lot
cheaper [a half ounce of tobacco lasts] four days.
Twenty cigarettes which costs over 30p more than half an
ounce of tobacco used to last me one day. Well 24
hours."

> Jason, smoker

John had reduced his tobacco consumption by smoking
cigars (See Section 4.13).

Nick's smoking was restricted because he only smoked when
socialising and those times were already restricted because of
money:

"[I smoke when] socialising really. There's quite a few
of me mates do it (...) Just when I'm sitting having a
drink."

> Nick, smoker

Although recreational activities for the unemployed were

minimal, they mostly managed to maintain some social contact:

> I go out, mostly I go out just for a drink like on
> Friday and Saturday nights when I get me money, you
> know. Just go out for a couple of pints like. (...) The
> other nights I sit in a lot of the time."
>
> John, smoker

Even without money there was a certain amount of 'free'
entertainment which Rob took advantage of:

> "[In the evening I] just go and see me mates (...)
> sometimes we go to the youth clubs (...) sometimes
> there's about two of us, sometimes three, sometimes
> there's up to ten of us."
>
> Rob, smoker

One of the unemployed, Jason, uncharacteristically
described an improvement in his social life since becoming
unemployed,

> "I get three nights out a week (....) mostly I go to the
> Turk's Head. But we go on a pub crawl everytime I go
> out. We always go around Peakside. [I drink] between
> five and eight pints. It depends how much money I've
> got, y'know. I enjoy it when I get out, y'know. But
> three nights a week when you're on the dole, it's not
> bad. (....) I'd say my social life's better now 'cause
> when I was working I used to come home, have some
> tea and have a nap - good rest - before I went out.
> Sometimes I'd go out grumpy. Sit there and drink.
> Enjoy me own company in some places, some pubs."
>
> Jason, smoker

Jason had many friends:

> "Most of [my friends] are employed (....) There can be
> about thirteen of us at once but mostly we stick down to
> about seven (....) most of them I've known since we were
> at school."

They all smoked and shared cigarettes. Jason had avoided the
cost involved in sharing cigarettes by switching to roll-ups:

> "[I don't share] not really because you see I smoke
> roll-ups and there's only one bloke (...) that smokes
> roll-ups."

In spite of this he did not exclude himself completely
from 'crashing':

> "There's one girl (...) she smokes tipped cigarettes
> and everytime - I might be able to cadge one off her but
> she'll always have to have a roll-up back, later on in
> the night."
>
> Jason, smoker

In contrast to Jason, Kevin, who was also unemployed,
had no friends. Since he was also without workmates, his social

contact was minimal:

> "[I don't have a social life] Not really, no, 'cause I never, like I said, I could never afford to go out. [I go out] well, for an odd pint. That's about it. [I] go out on me own (....) I had one friend, but he moved down to Derby."
>
> Darren, non-smoker

Darren had made some attempt to develop some interests at home:

> "[I] got some weights (...) its a course through a book [for] six months (...) I've got to about the third month. It's every Mondays, Wednesdays and Fridays. Sort of three days. Well, I've got the time as well.[I spend] 'bout an hour, an hour and a quarter doing it."
>
> Darren, non-smoker

Darren also used to collect football programmes from matches but now that he could not afford to go anymore, he collected records which he got from a mail order catalogue. Darren did not smoke.

5.9 Summary

This chapter confirmed that smoking played an important role in many of the young adults' social lives. This was especially true for those who were not involved in structured activities. For these young people, especially the young men who hung around "doing nothing" with their friends (cf Corrigan, 1978) smoking was a useful means of reaffirming social relationships within the group. The sharing of cigarettes seemed to strengthen the solidarity of the group. Those young people who could not share cigarettes in these situations often felt awkward.

The young people who were involved in organized social activities, especially sporting activities, were unlikely to smoke. The actual character of the activities not only structured the time but also provided strong social relationships. In addition, those who smoked realised the contradiction between this activity and continued participation in sports.

This was the period when the young men and women were establishing steady relationships (Levinson, 1978). For the women especially, this meant a limitation on wider social relationships. There also seemed to be a reduction in cigarette consumption among smokers. This was probably because only two were now involved in the sharing - the rounds were smaller.

6 Smoking and smokers

6.1 Introduction

Previous chapters have attempted to place smoking firmly within its immediate social and developmental context. However, the young people also discussed when they started smoking, what they thought of people who smoked, the experience of smoking and their attempts to stop smoking. To assist the part of the discussion concerned with the experience of smoking they were asked to distinguish between cigarettes and drugs. This chapter will consider some of these issues.

6.2 Starting to smoke

Most of the young men who smoked started to smoke when they were still at school. Brian recalled that pupils caught smoking at his school were disciplined by the teachers:

> "You got the cane for that at school (...) not allowed to smoke at our school, y'know. Smoking behind the bike shed - six of the best."
>
> Brian, smoker

However, this was little deterrent and they continued to smoke:

> "All go out and sit on the field in a big ring - silly when you think about it."
>
> Brian, smoker

George also recalled these smoking sessions at school:

> "When I was at school I did, yeah. Well, we all did, everybody did (...) or just about. All of us used to go, y'know, at break used to go on the field and have a fag just because you couldn't if you wanted to (...) loads of people around at one end of the field miles away from anyone with clouds of smoke going up."
>
> George, smoker

Some of the young men could recall their first experience of smoking:

> "When you first start to smoke, I mean its like because your other friends smoke (...) I can remember my first cigarette. I was sitting on a bus and someone gave me one so I took it (...) me and my mate (...) we wasn't taking anything down, y'know. We weren't smoking it properly, just sort of pleased to buy ten, y'know."
>
> Bill, smoker

Tom, a non-smoker, recalled experimenting with smoking in the Cadets:

> "I used to be in the Cadets (...) They was thirteen and that like. You started ... used to wake up at six in the morning, used to get a fag in before breakfast ...don't know how I could have done it (...) I hated it, youths of thirteen ... I'm against smoking, I am."
>
> Tom, non-smoker

A few of the young men had only started smoking after leaving school although they might have tried it once or twice at school. Dennis was particularly anti-smoking at school:

> "I didn't smoke at school, did I... like most kids (...) I used to get on to him [father] I watched films at school and I used to come home and say 'Ugh, I don't know how you can smoke', y'know. 'They turn your insides black and they kill you off' and all that. I was against it."
>
> Dennis, smoker

His father had even encouraged him to smoke:

> "The first cigarette I had was when I was about seven years old. I was with me Dad and all his mates (...) I coughed me guts up like."
>
> Dennis, smoker

However, Dennis remained a non-smoker until he left school:

> "When we first left school we started smoking Consulate (...) Them menthol fags were horrible so we packed that in but I got onto Park Drive which were really strong and I quite liked them (...) Y'know, I've never had no trouble like (...) I've never had to struggle smoking. If I'd have struggled I wouldn't have bothered."
>
> Dennis, smoker

Peter recalled how his cigarette consumption gradually increased during adolescence. He started:

> "About the same time as everybody else....first tried it when I was eight - didn't like it. Then really took up smoking when I was about twelve, and then seriously about sixteen."
>
> Peter, smoker

81

Others did not start smoking until later. Donald and Frank started shortly before leaving school:

> "I think I was about sixteen - quite late, friends in school. I can remember when we started - in the pictures, Embassy Regal, talk about it often."
>
> Donald, smoker

> "Started smoking just before me O levels when I was sixteen. About fifteen/sixteen I started (...) Yeah, somebody offered me a fag once when I was at school. I took it. I think I'd smoked about once or twice before. Never really carried on (...) When it came to doing exams started getting a bit nervous and somebody offered me another one - I took that (...) Then I started buying my own, then smoking just carried on from there."
>
> Frank, smoker

Sam, the young soldier, also did not smoke until he left school and entered the army (See Section 3.10).

Some of the non-smoking males tried smoking when young but disliked it immediately:

> "That's one thing I've never done (...) When I was about nine years, yes. This kid he says: 'Oi, start smoking'. I took one puff and it just about killed me. So I never bothered after that, just about killed me."
>
> Darren, non-smoker

Tony recalled pressure from his friends who used to tease him a lot:

> "You see I was the only one not smoking. I used to tell them, y'know, used to tell them the consequences of what it might do to you in future years."
>
> Tony, non-smoker

He claimed that one of the reasons he resisted this pressure was awareness of the health hazards:

> "The reason I never started smoking is when I was about fourteen I picked a packet up and it said on it 'Health warning: smoking can damage your health' and I never have, I never tried one since I read that headline."
>
> Tony, non-smoker

However, some of the non-smokers did smoke occasionally at school:

> "Only ... like you do when you're young. Your mates used to smoke.. its not many, y'know. Say, when you used to come out from school have one or two(...) mainly my last two years at school.I used to, y'know, smoke a couple a night."
>
> Terry, non-smoker

A few had never tried:

> "When I was at school (...) nobody ever pushed me into

it (...) I don't know whether I found some or got some from somewhere, y'know, ... handed them to me friends but I didn't really want any (...) so I gave them away really ... strange really, that .... perhaps if I took to it at school I'd have been smoking now."

Graham, non-smoker

Others were still experimenting:

"Well I took a drag or so, y'know, at Christmas like. Me mate offered me a fag so I just said yea, just for a joke. Of course he said 'Come on then, light it up then'. So 'e made me light it up and made me smoke a couple - I took a couple of drags, coughed."

Guy, non-smoker

Fewer of the young women recalled smoking at school. Those that did could be split into two groups. The first were those who smoked "down the field":

"I got caught smoking loads of time at school but it never made no impression on me (...) At breaktimes we used to go down the field and smoke. Or we used to go out of school at dinner, sneak down the street, y'know, hang around the shops smoking. The teachers would catch you and march you back in. The punishment they dealt out never made no impression on me whatsoever (..) I was always getting the cane for smoking or walking out of the school at dinner time."

Valerie, smoker

Judith was one of the few female non-smokers to mention others smoking at school. She did so in a derogatory manner:

"When I was at school all the kids that were from that sort of background used to go off behind the bike sheds or whatever and have a smoke at break because they thought it was big, y'know, really clever to do it."

Judith, non-smoker

It would seem that these girls who smoked within the school grounds did so partly as a display of their rejection of the world of school and of identification with the adult world outside school. Another group of girls were much more circumspect in their early smoking behaviour. They preferred to smoke well away from school so as not to threaten their relationship with the school while still identifying with the adult world, e.g.

"I was still at school but I didn't smoke at school. Never smoked at school. Everybody used to get caught and I said I'm not going to (...) I've seen a lot of people get caught. People would be prepared to risk it. I used to smoke on the way home."

Marion, smoker

The remaining young women who smoked, did not start until after leaving school:

83

"I didn't start 'til about three or four years ago- my last year at college which everybody smoked. There was probably an influence on me."

                                                    Tracey, smoker

These examples illustrate the importance of the school period in the establishment of smoking. Although most of the young people did not become regular smokers until after they left school most experimented with cigarettes while at school.

6.3 Smokers

Some earlier findings from the Derbyshire study (Bewley and Bland, 1978) found that among children there is a definite image of the smoker. Non-smokers viewed smokers as foolish and lazy and smokers were more likely to view themselves as foolish. There was evidence among the interviewees that such an image persisted into adulthood. Many of the non-smokers had a particularly negative view of smokers:

"I think perhaps people who are a bit on the thick side do tend to smoke more than a more intelligent person would (...) I think its back to joining in with what everybody else is doing. They don't know any better, sort of thing."

                                                    Katherine, non-smoker

"[Smokers are] a bit loud, rather working class. I think their money could be better spent."

                                                    Penny, non-smoker

Judith also felt that smoking was a more working class activity but the fact that her boyfriend's sister smoked was confusing:

"She's very clever, very bright, very pretty and I really like her and the fact that she smokes doesn't turn me off her at all, y'know. Yes, she's very clever, she's got a degree. I don't associate smoking with the working class at all or anything like that even though, I don't know, I have this idea that a lot more of them do smoke than say the middle class. "

                                                    Judith, non-smoker

The male non-smokers were less likely to refer to class in their description of the smoker and were generally less critical:

"They seem easy going people, the smokers, just ordinary, thats all".

                                                    Steven, non-smoker

The few smokers who did describe the smoker did, of course, provide generally favourble comments. Dennis thought smokers to be 'restless':

"[Smokers] like to keep something going. Like if they're not smoking a fag they're probably supping a cup of tea or chewing a sandwich or eating a boiled sweet or chewing some chewing gum. They're sort of restless, y'know. I won't say they're energetically fit, rearing to go, but they're just, y'know, restless"

Dennis, smoker

Whether or not someone smoked seemed to play an important part in selecting a boy - or girl-friend. Many of the young male non-smokers particularly disliked female smokers:

"Its alright 'til you're kissing them. No, I don't like smoking, think its unfeminine. I don't like to see women smoking."

Terry, non-smoker

"... it puts me off, y'know, when I see them smoke. At first, y'know, you've taken up with a girl and you think "Ooh she's nice" and then she puts a cigarette in her mouth and you think 'Ugh', y'know. I've been out with one girl that smokes and it was horrible, really."

Ken, non-smoker

It wasn't only the bad breath which put these young men off but the whole general image of the female smoker. Len explained this:

"I don't think it looks quite bad if men do it (...) for some reason (...) I don't know if thats being funny about it, whatever. I just think it looks wrong... and walking out, walking down the street either with a cigarette in the hand or one stuck in the corner of the mouth all the time (...) I don't think men (...) walk along the street quite the same (...) in the mouth. If you know what I mean. They walk along the streets holding one in their hands(...) When I saw someone she was riding a bike and she was smoking with both hands on the handlebars (...) I don't think that looks very good, y'know...I don't suppose it would if a man did it either but its just that I tend to pick up on women (...) a bit more."

Len, non-smoker

Hilary, a smoker, seemed aware of this negative image of the female smoker held by some people. She tried to avoid being typecast:

"I never smoked out, I thought it looked disgusting(...) I don't smoke a great deal in the pub unless there's other girls smoking 'cause I don't think it looks right. And I don't smoke if I'm walking along the street on my own."

Hilary, smoker

The male smokers accepted female smoking:

"Unless they're pregnant (...) just for health reasons (...) doesn't bother me at all."

Peter, smoker

So too did some male non-smokers but only conditionally:

> "If she was nice looking and I wanted to go out with her then I'd go out with her. Its as simple as that(...) If she didn't smoke it would be even better."
>
> Graham, non-smoker

The female non-smokers also disliked boyfriends who smoked:

> "....me previous boyfriend smoked a lot and I didn't like it. And then when we finished I went out with this one. I said I would never go out with anyone who smoked again...When you come home you come in you can smell your clothes. You smell horrible. People tell you your hair smells (...) Its not very nice. And you find that if you want to wear them again you have got to have them washed or else you want to go out smelling and then you feel a bit dirty."
>
> Kim, non-smoker

The social conotations of smoking were clearly revealed in these examples. Although the image of the smoker was not fixed, whether or not a person smoked was often taken into consideration by the young adults when forming an impression of someone.

6.4 Cigarettes and drugs

It would seem that one of the reasons for the difficulty in quitting smoking is the physically addictive qualities of the substances in tobacco smoke (Royal College of Physicians, 1983). As such, tobacco can be classed as a drug, and cigarette smokers treated as drug addicts. However, the young smokers in our study were loath to make this equation:

> "I suppose it is a drug. I don't think it is. I just think of it as a fag. I suppose it is because its addictive and all that. I don't think of it as a drug, y'know. I just think of it as fags."
>
> George, smoker

Both smokers and non-smokers differentiated cigarettes from drugs on at least four dimensions: health consequences, addictiveness, acceptability and effect. However, the extent of the difference between cigarettes and drugs along these dimensions varied between smokers and non-smokers.

Smokers and non-smokers agreed that, at least in the short-term, drugs were more harmful than cigarettes:

> "Other drugs actually do more damage, y'know, in the long run to your health and they're more of, more of a hazard - real drugs."
>
> Terry, non-smoker

> "I think other drugs are more harming in a way... short-term wise (...) I think cigarette smoking, I think it is dangerous to your health but I think its a

86

long-term, very long-term thing, y'know."

Sam, smoker

But smokers emphasised that the intrinsic danger of drug taking was the ease with which one could accidentally overdose. Smoking was a more controllable risk:

"Say if I'd had three fags, one after the other, it wouldn't cause me any damage, would it? Say if I was on drugs and I took a bit extra it would kill me from an overdose."

Rob, smoker

"They say that cigarettes can kill you, smoking can kill you. But drugs I mean its easy, easy to take an ovedose of drugs and then you're dead like that. I mean it takes years to kill you smoking."

Emma, smoker

Some smokers suggested that whilst drugs were often impure and, so, dangerous, tobacco was pure and so less dangerous:

"Smoking cigarettes you know that you're smoking the original things, aren't you?"

Bill, smoker

"Well cigarettes - you know they're the real things."

Jason, smoker

Besides harmfulness, the other most frequently used dimension was addictiveness. The non-smokers were quite forthright in characterising cigarettes as addictive:

"Because people just get addicted to them like any drug you get addicted to after taking for so long. Its obvious (...) A lot of people are on tranquilisers and things like that which you can get addicted to. You get the impression you can't live without it, y'know, like people do with smoking."

Helen, non-smoker

"Well I think people find it hard to pack in. Its like a drug that ... once you start its hard to come off like. Most people say, 'I can't pack in I tried to pack in but I started again.'"

Barry, non-smoker

Some of the smokers did likewise:

"I'm addicted to them (...) I've only smoked about five years so I suppose they are in a way [drugs]."

Brian, smoker

However, many of the smokers were more circumspect. They either underplayed the addictiveness of cigarettes or they emphasised that addiction only occurred after regular and prolonged use:

"I think cigarettes are somthing which you can give up

87

reasonably easily. I mean its very difficult if you've been smoking for a long time but I think its very different to [...] drug addiction."

Alison, smoker

"Its easier to get addicted to these other drugs. I mean just from what I've read and that...It's easier to get addicted to them (...) They're not addictive, I don't think, cigarettes, but they can be. I think they're more... its more habit-forming, y'know, something to do with your hands."

Sam, smoker

The smokers were attempting to distinguish between what they saw as physical addiction, as with drugs, and social psychological addiction as with smoking.

One dimension which was not used by smokers was that concerned with the social acceptability or legality of smoking. To those non-smokers who considered smoking similar to drug-taking the main difference was social acceptability:

"The difference really between smoking and other drugs is very small (...) even though I sort of frown on smoking and things and I frown on drugs I think the difference is very [small]. Its probably just social, social attitude, really. It seems odd in some ways that one should be against the law."

Matthew, non-smoker

"You can buy cigarettes more easily than you can buy drugs. Its sort of a very common thing to buy. Lots more people do it - smoke, that is (...) whereas you've got to (...) go out and get drugs, you've got to do loads of things for that (...) I think more people would turn to drugs if they knew how to get hold of them."

Katherine, non-smoker

The smokers probably avoided the use of this dimension as a means of avoiding classification of themselves as drug-users. However, Sam, a light smoker, did refer to the relative cost of cigarettes which he related to their acceptability:

"...they're [drugs] more expensive to get hold of. So...a cigarette you can go down to the shop and buy a cigarette and think no more of it, y'know."

Sam, smoker

The fourth dimension was the different effect of drugs and cigarettes on the user. The non-smoker tended to denigrate the limited effect of smoking cigarettes:

"Well cigarettes, as far as I can see, there's no effect, so ... I mean there must be something there because people can't give up but, y'know, you need a lot to get an effect."

Barry, non-smoker

"Some people smoke to ease their nerves which I've heard. Although it must be true I guess its just that you could never believe it possible."

Roger, non-smoker

"At least when you're taking drugs you're getting something out of it. You can, you can sort of feel it, can't you? When you're on drugs and get high on that but on cigarettes they just calm you down, but you don't, don't think you feel anything after that

Susan, non-smoker

Smokers, on the other hand emphasised the immediate pleasurable effect of smoking which although limited were much less likely than drugs to be unpleasant:

"....a cigarette gives you satisfaction, doesn't it? Calms your nerves, I suppose. But dope just makes you, like, drunk. Probably a cheap way of getting drunk, really."

Ron, smoker

"....cigarettes is a mild drug basically. All it does is give you tingling effect, sensation (...) Thats about it, calms your nerves."

Brian, smoker

Dennis was particularly alarmed at the supposed effect of drugs:

"It can have bad side effects. Like, you can see frightening things like a little...if you looked at a little spider in one of them hallucinations it could be a giant spider and it could frighten you 'til you're dead like, y'know, things like that. It's something I'm not bothered with, y'know, that other world. I'm happy with the world I'm in, y'know."

Dennis, smoker

Tracey thought that unlike drugs the effect of smoking cigarettes was largely psychological not physical:

"They don't really put you under any influence and they're not...you don't get high smoking them. That would be the difference I'd draw. That you consciously go out and take other drugs to either bring yourself up or bring yourself down. Whereas with cigarettes - you don't smoke a cigarette to get high. I smoke a cigarette because I enjoy it. That would be the line I draw between the two."

Tracey, smoker

One interesting sex difference in the young people's discussion on drugs was that whereas none of the young men referred to pharmaceuticals several of the young women did, often in a very negative manner:

"No chance, not on your life [try drugs] I won't even

take nerve tablets when I were poorly. I wouldn't take them, no. Like paracetamols, I mean, theres all them great long words. I don't know what they mean - could be something thats doing good for one thing and rotting something else."

Hilary, smoker

Some of the non-smokers when discussing the difference between cigarettes and drugs tended to view them as types of tranquilisers:

"Say people have got problems and they do smoke, perhaps a nervous problem, and they smoke because of that (....) its not as strong as a drug. It can sort of help that person with perhaps the nerve problem just by smoking a cigarette (...) A cigarette might solve a small problem whereas people who think they've got a very big problem they might turn to drugs (...) as an escape. Well, I don't know much about drugs at all but things I have heard - it makes you happier, it makes you feel you haven't got any problems."

Katherine, non-smoker

This young woman seems to be suggesting that some people need cigarettes or drugs as a means of coping with everyday problems. One young mother emphasised particularly this value in smoking:

"I work them out, y'know. I try to work the problems out and if I just can't make ends meet I think 'Oh bugger it', throw it down, have a cigarette, y'know. I think 'Oh, forget it. I'll try it another day', y'know. I sit down and have a cigarette. Actually with me a cigarette seems to cure everything, everthing I do, y'know - have a cigarette it will cure it, y'know."

Sarah, smoker

However, not all smokers thought smoking had a tranquilizing effect:

"Calms me down? I haven't really looked on smoking like that. (....) No, I just do it and that's that."

Nick, smoker

A contradictory flavour seemed to enter into the young people's definition of drugs. Whilst the non-smokers defined cigarettes as drugs, the smokers rather avoided such a definition. Although they found it difficult to distinguish cigarettes clearly from drugs the smokers were reluctant to make the equation lest it would imply that they accepted the definition of themselves as drug-takers.

6.5 Stopping smoking

Related to our finding that some of the smokers felt they were addicted to smoking was our finding that many of them had failed in their repeated attempts to stop smoking:

"At first, when I first started smoking I had one 'cause, well, I hadn't had a fag for ages so I'll have one. But now if I don't have a fag for ages I'll be going 'Golly, I've got no fags' and I'll start panicking. I tried to pack up about three times, didn't work (...) Can't do it. I've got no will power (...) I've tried it. I've tried it. Pauline, the woman who sits next to me, she takes me fags off me but I'll go and borrow one of somebody else and I'll say 'I'll give you one back when Pauline gives me me fags'. So it does work, especially with people smoking, y'know, with you at work."

Hilary, smoker

"The trouble with me, I can't pack in smoking. I've tried and I've tried four times. I can't pack it in. When I get upset, its my weak point sort of thing, have a cigarette, calm me down."

Sarah, smoker

Some of the young men did have success for various reasons. George had almost given up smoking:

"At the most I have one a day now apart from, y'know, if I drink I have a couple more because when I drink I just, I don't know, I just feel like a fag. But I used to smoke about ten a day, at one time (...) About first year at work..at school, smoked a bit there but I just got fed up with it really. The taste in my mouth after used to bug me, I think. Then, y'know, just the thought of going to buy them. Its not the money but its the bother of going to buy them. Can't be bothered. If I go into a pub I just, I don't know if its having a drink or being with everybody but, y'know, it just makes me have a fag...so I scrounge one."

George, smoker

Peter managed to give up for six months but started again:

"Basically 'cause I put on too much weight and I was saving up to go abroad as well and I knew that once we arrived on the flight the duty-frees and everything would come around and I intended smoking anyway on me holiday so I just started again."

Peter, smoker

Both Derek and Mick were more successful. Derek had just stopped:

"I don't know.. why I stopped smoking. The other night, I seen that programme on tele, y'know... I'd been thinking about it for a while, seeing that programme."

Derek, ex-smoker

Mick was the most successful. He thought the reason why was:

"....pressure from me Dad to tell you the truth (....) I

was in the Navy. I couldn't do it at home. I'd feel
guilty. The other one was cost (...) spending 90p a day.
It was ridiculous 'cause I wasn't getting paid that much
at all."

Mick, ex-smoker

Fewer of the young women reported success. Vicki managed to
stop for a few months:

"My boss (...) went for acupuncture to stop smoking and
I went as well but it didn't work (...) It was alright
to start with but I suppose it is a bit of a new
thing (...) After a bit it just got so it bored me.
It just didn't work anymore. I went back for a booster
and they did it all again and I suppose I didn't
really want to stop 'cause me boss really wanted to..
he'd been smoking 40 a day for 20 years and he just
stopped but I lasted 2 1/2 months before I had a
cigarette (...) I can remember that. It made me dizzy a
bit (...) I put on 1 1/2 stone as well. That was
mainly the reason....the weight. Couldn't get into any
of my clothes."

Vicki, smoker

While Christine was off them for two weeks:

"Me Mums always on at me about it (...) I gave up for a
fortnight and then I started again and I want to give up
again and I'm going to have another go."

Christine, smoker

This interesting sex difference could imply that smoking is
assuming greater value to young women than to young men.

One factor which might encourage smokers to continue smoking is
their estimate of the changing prevalence of smoking amongst
their peers. The young people tended to view smoking as being on
the decline. This was the case among both non-smokers and
smokers:

"I think meself its... I think its going out, smoking,
round our age anyway (...) I've noticed that quite a few
of my friends round my age don't smoke at all."

Graham, non-smoker

"I think less people smoke now, don't they? Fred, I used
to work with, he really smokes a lot, he does. Its when
he asked for a light and nobody had a light and I
realized nobody smoked around me."

George, smoker

Despite this generally optimistic view about a decline
in the prevalence of smoking most young people were
pessimistic about the eventual elimination of smoking
altogether. Both smokers and non-smokers were generally
agreed that smokers lacked the motivation to stop smoking.
They had been smoking too long to abandon the habit of a
lifetime:

> "You get stuck on it and people don't wanna get over it. Y'know, they can't be bothered to try and get over it(...) They get caught on it and can't be bothered to try and get off it."
>
> Guy, non-smoker

The smokers especially emphasized the potential plight of the old person being discouraged from smoking. They seemed almost to be attempting to make a plea for clemency which would include themselves:

> "There'll always be people smoking (...) Its what they want to do. You can't stop them by law, can you? I mean how can you tell a 65 year old man who's smoked all his life, who's just retiring, now he's got nothing to do on his hands: 'O.K. you're not going to smoke anymore'. He's going to do it more because he's got nothing to do on his hands. He's bound to smoke. You can't stop him."
>
> Dennis, smoker

Some young women thought that smoking was on the increase or would increase in the future:

> "....there's more and more young people smoking now than what I can remember. I think its mainly just on the increase I suppose."
>
> Vicki, smoker

However, the general perception of the trend in the prevalence of smoking was downward.

6.6 Summary

This section of the study confirmed the importance of the secondary school period as the time when experimentation with cigarettes is widespread among young people. Some of the reasons for this were outlined in the introductory chapter. These young people emphasized that they began smoking with their friends. The adoption of smoking was part of the shared experience of growing up. It was something you did with your friends.

Now that they had entered early adulthood these young people were identifying suitable partners for marriage. The image presented by individual members of the opposite sex was an important factor in deciding whether a relationship was initiated. Many of the non-smokers considered smoking an indication of an unsuitable character. Women who smoked were especially frowned upon.

The young people distinguished cigarettes from drugs along four dimensions: health hazards, addictiveness, acceptability and effect. The extent to which the young people used these dimensions depended upon whether they smoked themselves.

Despite their avoidance of the label drug-addict many of the young people admitted that they found it very difficult to give up smoking - they were addicted to it in a social and psychological sense. This form of addiction was no less powerful than pharmacological addiction. There was a suggestion that this was especially the case among the young women.

7 Smoking and health

7.1 Introduction

The medical definition of illness emphasizes pathological changes in human physiology. Since cigarette smoking is associated with such changes it follows that smoking causes illness and should therefore be discouraged. However, to the layman health and illness are not simply defined in terms of physiology. Rather they have various social and psychological dimensions (cf. Herzlich, 1974).

The young people in this study were asked to provide their definitions of health and illness, the causes of ill-health and the methods which should be used to maintain health. From this information it was then possible to identify how much a threat to their health they perceived smoking to be.

7.2 Definition of health

For both smokers and non-smokers the primary definition of health was fitness. Almost every male referred to fitness when asked to define health, e.g.:

> "Its being basically sound, y'know, fit"
> > Terry, non-smoker

> "A reasonable fitness both mentally and physically."
> > Mick, ex-smoker

The young women used this term less frequently although it was still the most popular definition of health for them, e.g.

> "Keep fit."
> > Marion, smoker

> "Being as fit as you possibly can be"
> > Linda, non-smoker

Both the young men and women usually extended this definition to emphasize its active dimension. Fitness was perceived as the ability to perform tasks - it was not exceptional rather it was normal. A few examples of this normality were:

"Being able to run for the bus without losing your breath."

Jason, smoker

"To be able to run up the stairs without having to pant at the top.... to be able to go places, do things you want to do and not be able to tell when you've done it."

Helen, non-smoker

Several of the young men in their attempts to underline the normality of health distinguished athleticism from fitness. Being athletic was not normal. Dennis explained the difference:

"I'm superfit. I mean I'm pretty big here, but I can sort of look after myself. I can do a days work without feeling too tired. Y'know, I'd say I'm fit enough to do my job. I wouldn't say I'm a sportsman. I'm not athletic. I'm fairly healthy. I wouldn't say I'm, y'know, an athletic person but I'm sort of fit enough to cope with everyday needs that I need to do like"

Dennis, smoker

Roger also tried to differentiate between normal health and athleticism although he termed the latter fitness:

"Healthy's easy really - just go through the routine of eating, going to sleep. But to keep fit, that's, running, squash, sports in general."

Roger, non-smoker

The other main dimension used in these young people's definitions of health was the state of a person's body and mind. This dimension can be considered the passive definition of health:

"I suppose its being in a situation where there's nothing physically or mentally wrong with you."

Frank, smoker

"I suppose it depends on, y'know, your body an' that. Er, I know some illnesses can be caused by the job you're doing and that but most of it depends on how your body's built and that, y'know, if you're immune to certain things."

Terry, non-smoker

There was a suggestion that the young women used this definition more frequently than did the young men:

"Healthy... well its physical and its mental."

Christine, smoker

"A person not being ill. Not being ill very often."
Tracey, smoker

Illness was the reverse of health: it was a reduction in ability to perform everyday acts or a deterioration of a person's body or mind.

7.3 Causes of ill-health

Since the young men emphasized the active dimension of health in their definitions it would be expected that they would refer to those factors which restrict activity in their discussion of the causes of ill-health. There was some evidence that this was the case. Consider two examples.

Ron was a seasonal fairground worker. During the summer he worked in a coastal resort and felt very healthy. But during the winter months when he was unemployed in Peakside he felt some inertia setting in:

"I was fit as hell when I was at Bellstown , y'know. I lost a lot of weight and what not and built me muscles up - its all cutting and scraping, woodwork, concrete. Down there I don't mind [running] along the sea and back. I don't mind that a bit... but now I've come back here and I haven't got no job or doing anything. I've put on a pound and that, but that's what happens - you get it in the winter, you lose it in the summer."
Ron, smoker

John, another smoker, was currently unemployed. He felt that his enforced inactivity reduced his health or, more particularly, gave him 'flab'.

For these young men illness meant interference with the ability to perform everyday activities. Since smoking did not do this it was not considered a serious threat to health by many smokers:

"I like smoking now and I don't care if it is rotting me insides. I don't feel any worse. I mean perhaps I might get out of puff running up the street a bit more but then again I'm not an athletic person. I'm more muscley for me job rather than run up and down the street every two minutes(....) In the job I do I don't get out of puff but probably running up the road all day I'd get out of puff dead fast which someone else who doesn't smoke probably wont"
Dennis, smoker

But Mick, an ex-smoker, remembered how smoking had started to interfere with his everyday life:

"The more you smoke the worse you get (....) When I smoked I never went above twenty a day (....) It got me running up stairs - terrible. You'd have to have a fag to start with to go up and one to finish."
Mick, ex-smoker

Similarly, Hilary who had recently adopted smoking was aware
of the ill- effects it had on her life:

> "..before I could run (....) before when I was in the
> band I never smoked and then when I went back and
> started playing again, I get out of breath so easily."
>
> Hilary, smoker

Related to the passive definition of health was the
suggeston that ill-health was inherited, the person had little
control over his or her health:

> "I suppose it depends on, y'know, your body and that. I
> know some illnesses can be caused by the job you're
> doing and that, but most of it depends on how your
> body's built and that, if you're immune to certain
> things"
>
> Terry, non-smoker

To some young people this fatalistic explanation meant that
smoking was of little importance in the development of illness:

> "Smoking [doesn't kill] everybody (...) It can cause
> cancer but you've already got cancer there, haven't you?
> Or so they say."
>
> Emma, smoker

> "You get some people who're smoking who're always
> unhealthy and you get some people who smoke all the time
> and seem to be alright."
>
> Jim, non-smoker

The effect of age on health was also taken into
consideration by these young people when assessing the
possible harm of smoking. According to Dennis children should
not smoke as their bodies were too delicate but adults like him
had strong bodies which could resist the ill-effects of
smoking. However, with old age comes the inevitable
deterioration of the body and the consequent ill-health:

> "When you get older you get them [illnesses] don't you?"
>
> George, smoker

While young people could be unconcerned about their health,
with increasing age they would have to take precautions. Rob,
a smoker, noticed how not only the body deteriorated with age
but also that consequent reduced activity could lead to
smoking and further ill-health:

> "Well eventually you get...I mean....I don't see as it
> matters when you're young but when you start getting
> older you just stay about in the house all day eating
> and smoking and it can cause damage to your heart."
>
> Rob, smoker

Those young people who considered health a mental state
emphasized the importance of psychological factors in the
development of illness:

> "....it can sometimes be your state of mind, apart from the obvious diseases that make you sick. How you feel. If you feel low and depressed it can make you ill in different ways...or if you feel happy and confident then you feel better."
>
> Emma, smoker

Smoking to this type of person may actually be perceived as an aid to lifting depression and so, in their eyes, an aid to health.

These few examples illustrate how smoking was perceived as being of only limited harm when considered within the young people's own definitions of health and illness. A few of the smokers denied altogether the potential physical harm of smoking:

> "From time to time [health risks] cross my mind but there's no proof and whilst there's no proof it doesn't really bother me too much.... well, occasionaly it does, yes. It will get to me and then I'll sort of slow down a bit and then I'll just go back to normal again."
>
> Christine, smoker

Many of the young smokers excused their smoking on the grounds that they did not smoke sufficient cigarettes to cause themselves harm:

> "The little I smoke it doesn't really bother me ... 'cause I read a book once about 'Do you smoke between one and ten? you've got more chance of being knocked down,' or something. I don't know if that's true. It sort of stuck in my mind see. I just think its like anything,...if you don't go over the top you're not too bad, are you?"
>
> George, smoker

Others continued to smoke since the visible effects were as yet minimal:

> "If I have a cold it never goes like most people onto their chest and to a terrible cough. But maybe if there came a day when I was coughing like a dirty old man, y'know, I probably would want to stop."
>
> Tracey, smoker

But the effects of long-term smoking did cause concern to some smokers:

> "I'm always thinking, 'Oh well, I can stop soon, I don't have to smoke.' But I do. But when I look at my Dad and he sort of coughs in the morning and gets bad chests in the winter (...) it really worries me when I look at my parents."
>
> Alison, smoker

The non-smokers seemed aware of the ill-effects of smoking:

> "I think [smoking] does damage your health. Most [smokers] if they get a cough and cold they always seem

99

to be a lot worse than if you don't smoke."
Kim, non-smoker

The non-smokers, unlike the smokers, correctly identified the physical damage caused by smoking. However, the smokers either generally denied any harmful effects or claimed that they were not applicable in their case.

7.4 Health maintenance

Most of the young people, both smokers and non-smokers, agreed on the necessity to engage in various activities to maintain their health. The character of these activities was not only related to the two dimensions of health but also to the sex of the young people. It has been found that the self-concept of late adolescent boys is related to their physical effectiveness whereas the self-concept of late adolescent girls is based on assessment of their own physical attractiveness (Lerner and Karabenick, 1974). In this study the young men's health maintenance was particularly concerned with activities such as body building and weight training which would aid the development of the ideal muscular male form. On the other hand, the young women preferred keep-fit classes and diet.

The character of the young men's health maintenance activities was also related to the fitness definition of health. There were many examples of these male/fitness activities:

"I march miles and miles. I cycle (....) Thats why I don't buy a car (...) If you buy a car you get lazy."
Bill, smoker

"I do press-ups every night and every morning (...) When I'm at University I go jogging everyday."
Matthew, non-smoker

Although the smokers did participate in these health maintenance activites they were less likely to do so in an organised form such as through belonging to a club. They preferred a more casual approach which emphasized the immediate pleasure of the activity rather than any aim of improving health.

The contrast in the attitude of male smokers and non-smokers towards involvement in regular exercise can be seen in the comments of Tim and of Brian and Frank. Tim, a non-smoker, was particularly fanatical about health maintenance:

"Health is my life really. Its the way I see life(...) I've been into it for three years, two or three years now seriously. And every time I lay off I think I'm unfit. I feel unfit and I don't like that feeling. I just have to keep going on, keeping fit, doing training. Its hard work."
Tim, non-smoker

On the other hand Brian and Frank, both smokers had recently given up involvement in such fitness/exercise programmes:

"I used to do body-building but I packed it up.(...) I'm sorry I gave it up. I'm thinking about starting it up again. Means I've got to pack up cigarettes as well as beer."

Brian, smoker

"....at one time I was doing press-ups, press-ups and things like that(...) I suppose it must have been doing something but it didn't seem to work. I went through a stage when I was quite happy and I was seriously thinking of taking up jogging and those things. It never materialized only got to thinking stage."

Frank, smoker

The young women also engaged in exercise to maintain health although to a lesser extent than they used diet or weight control. It is noticeable that their exercises were not strenuous but more of the keep-fit type which are also related to weight control:

"I exercise and thats about it. Just sort of keep fit things, y'know, touching me toes. .... I used to go jogging a lot. I've packed up a lot now though. I don't have time."

Hilary, smoker

"I try to keep fit, to keep my body fit by doing Keep-Fit on Monday and Tuesday."

Tracey, smoker

All these young women were smokers. It may be that for some women both Keep-Fit and smoking are indications of a general concern for body image.

For most of the young women health maintenance meant diet and weight control - essential for maintaining the ideal female shape:

"I try to have a balanced diet which is also basically to do with watching your weight but its still to do with your health as well."

Tracey, smoker

Smoking was seen by some of these young women as an aid to weight control - an aid to being healthy:

"[Smoking] stopped me biting me nails and it made me lose a lot of weight as well."

Hilary, smoker

Christine was reluctant to quit smoking lest she gain weight:

"Mightn't be a bad idea [to stop smoking] as long as I don't put my weight back on again."

Christine, smoker

Vicki stopped smoking for two and a half months but started again in an effort to control her weight:

101

> "I put on half a stone as well. That was mainly, mainly the reason... the weight, couldn't get into any of my clothes."
>
> Vicki, smoker

Related to the definition of health as a state of mind was the view that health maintenance was partly psychological. To keep healthy, Emma thought people should:

> "Get out and enjoy themselves, don't let things get them down. Just take life as it comes, I'd say, but some people take it too seriously. They worry over things that aren't worth worrying about."
>
> Emma, smoker

Vicki had a similar view of health which she defined as:

> "Keeping going. I have to be really, really ill to stop in or anything like that. I don't get ill very often. I think its because when I feel as if I'm getting bad I'll always say 'You're not going to be bad' (...) I just keep myself going and going and I think thats one of the best medicines you can have."
>
> Vicki, smoker

It was not suprising that these two women did not perceive smoking as a threat to their health. Admittedly Matthew, a non-smoker, adopted a similar view:

> "It's a very mental matter. It's a lot to do with the mind. In some ways if you try and stay alert and keep happy you're probably a bit more resilient."
>
> Matthew, non-smoker

All of these examples suggest that there is a complex relationship between smoking and health maintenance. It was not simply that people who smoked were not interested in maintaining their health. Rather the smokers seemed to prefer a different kind of health maintenance. The male smokers preferred the more casual forms of physical exercise while the female smokers were particularly concerned about their weight.

7.5 Attitude to health

An important factor in deciding to what extent the young adults engaged in various health maintenance activities was their general attitude to health. There was a suggestion that the smokers held a more fatalistic attitude:

> "Well you can get killed crossing the road, y'know. Besides, its not as if I can see it killing me, y'know. Its not as if I can see slowly, Oh, thats another nail in your coffin, like. Its something, y'know, you either die of cancer or you don't, y'know. You all die one day."
>
> Dennis, smoker

Ron thought that health maintenance was unnecessary:

102

"Smoking don't help, does it? Exercise helps, eating the
right food, I suppose. But then again I smoke and I
don't do all that much exercise now and I eat chips and
everything and I've never had nowt wrong with me."
                                        Ron, smoker

Whether or not these young people engaged in health maintenance
was partly dependent on their attitude to health. In
general, the non-smokers valued health highly whereas the
smokers were less concerned:

"It matters a lot if you haven't got your health. You
can't really get on with your life. If its not one
hundred per cent then life becomes difficult for you. If
you've got bad health or if something's gone wrong with
you you tend not to do everything, just because of that
health."
                                    Mary, non-smoker

"I'm not bothered about health."
                                    George, smoker

Peter typified the carefree attitude of some of the smokers:

"Me mates say I don't fear death just the way I cross
the roads."
                                        Peter, smoker

However, he did accept that in later years he might change his
views and become concerned about his smoking but:

"At the moment it just doesn't bother me (...) It might
but who knows."
                                        Peter, smoker

Brian was also quite dismissive of various health risks and in
particular of smoking as a health risk:

"Put a fag through a tissue paper - you can see all the
yellow tar thats going to your lungs - but it doesn't
really bother me."
                                        Brian, smoker

Admittedly in the face of repeated warnings about the health
hazards of smoking some of the smokers felt concern:

"I know the risks (...) and (....) it does worry me, not
that much. I don't really know why actually."
                                        Donald, smoker

"I just feel guilty about it.. y'know... all these
things on tele and that... I just can't see why I do
it(...) its just filthy aint it?.... I mean.... all this
talk about cancer and that... what smoke does and that."
                                        Nick, smoker

These two smokers are what McKennell and Thomas (1967) termed
the 'dissonant' smokers: those whose smoking behaviour
conflicted with their attitudes and beliefs about smoking. Both

these young men were actively involved in social activities where a lot of their smoking took place. The health hazards of smoking about which they expressed concern when alone were of little consequence when weighed against the immediate social value of 'crashing' with their friends.

7.6 Summary

The young people largely defined health and illness in personal and social terms as well as in terms of physical and mental processes. This is similar to the findings of several other investigations (e.g. Herzlich, 1974; Blaxter and Paterson 1983). The young men, in particular, preferred an activity definition of health. In accord with this many of them participated in active physical pursuits to maintain their level of health/fitness. However, those who smoked tended to adopt a much more casual approach to their involvement in such activities. This helped to conceal any reduction in their level of fitness due to smoking.

Many of the young women took part in keep-fit activities and were careful about their diet. Besides being aspects of health maintenance these activities were also aimed at maintaining physical attractivness. The value of smoking as an aid to weight control was specifically mentioned by several of the young women.

PART III
THE SURVEY

8 Design of the survey

8.1 Introduction

Analysis of the interviews conducted with the 49 young adults suggested that smoking has a variety of different meanings when considered within the context of the young peoples' lives. In particular, smoking was used by the young adults as a means of structuring time and of establishing and reinforcing social relationships. However, the importance of these meanings for explaining smoking in different situations was often unclear. In summarising the interviews various speculative relationshipos have been suggested. This part of the study considers in more detail the relationships between these meanings and the character of the social context within which the young adults live and work. The method adopted in this part of the research was the survey.

Of course the survey is limited in the quality of information it can provide about a psychosocial phenomenon such as smoking. In view of this, the findings of the survey need to be read in conjunction with those of the interview study to obtain a fuller understanding of smoking among young adults.

8.2 Feasibility study

It was decided to use as our sample of young adults those young people who had participated in the original Derbyshire Study between 1974 and 1978 when they were aged between 11-12 and 15-16 years. The membership of this cohort was drawn from all the secondary schools in Derbyshire and provides a good representation of young people. Further details of the composition of the cohort are given elsewhere (Banks et al., 1978; Murray et al., 1984).

However, there were certain problems involved in using the members of this cohort as our sample. First, the survey had to be conducted by post using mailing addresses provided by the schools. However, it was possible that since reaching school-leaving age in 1978 many of the young people had changed addresses or had married and changed their names. In addition, the original survey had been conducted in the schools where there was a certain amount of compulsion about answering the questionnaire. It was possible that given the chance in a postal survey many of the cohort members would refuse to participate. Both these factors would reduce the response rate.

In order to gauge the possible response rate to a detailed survey of this cohort a feasibility study was conducted in 1981 when the young people were aged 18-19 years. A brief questionnaire and return envelope was posted to those addresses available from the 1978 school registers. In that year the cohort consisted of 7295 individuals. The questionnaire asked the young people to check and correct their address if they had moved house or name if they had married. In addition, it included six questions on their employment status, living arrangements, smoking behaviour and health status. A message was printed on the envelope advising the recipient to forward it to the addressee if he or she had moved. If the recipient did not have a forwarding address they should return it to the sender. Three reminders were dispatched to the non-respondents at intervals of three weeks.

Of the 7295 questionnaires distributed 678 (9.3%) were returned by the Post Office or current householder indicating that the addressee had moved and that they were unaware of the new address. Of the remaining 6617 potential respondents, completed questionnaires were returned from 3894 (58.8%) after the first postage, a further 1039 (15.7%) after a reminder had been sent, a further 540 (8.2%) after a second reminder and a further 239 (3.6%) after third reminder. Thus, of the 6617 potential respondents 5712 (86.3%) returned completed questionnaires.

The response to this feasibility study confirmed that it was possible to trace and obtain the cooperation of a large proportion of the young people who had participated in the original Derbyshire study. In view of this it was decided to base our survey on this sample of young adults.

8.3 The main survey

The questionnaire used in the main survey was developed from the accounts provided by the young people in the interview study. Except for a few questions, the questionnaire was structured with the respondents being required to tick the appropriate box to indicate their answer to the question.

The questionnaire was designed to collect information on the following:

a) general details: sex, social class, marital status;
b) work: type of job, characteristics of job;
c) leisure: leisure activities, friendships, drinking;
d) smoking: consumption, reasons for smoking, sharing of cigarettes;
e) psychological factors: how time is perceived and managed;
f) health: health status, health-related behaviours, respiratory symptoms.

A pilot version of this questionnaire was sent to a sample of 20 of the young people who had participated in the interview study. An accompanying letter explained that a research worker would subsequently call to collect the questionnaire. On calling, the investigator invited the young adult to identify any problems in the questionnaire. Together they went through each of the questions allowing the investigator to identify any misinterpretations and whether the alternative responses to the various questions were sufficient. Using this information a final version of the questionnaire was developed (see Appendix).

In March 1984 a copy of the final questionnaire was sent to the 5712 individuals now aged 21-22 years who had responded to the feasibility study in 1981. In addition, questionnaires were also sent to the 1583 individuals, who had not responded in 1981 either because they had moved house or they did not wish to participate. They were included in the main survey in the hope that the current householder had subsequently obtained a forwarding address or the individual named might reassess his or her decision not to respond. Finally, 248 individuals from one school who had participated in the original 1974-78 survey but whose addresses were not available in 1981 were also included in the sample since an address file had subsequently been made available. This provided a grand total of 7543 as our possible sample size. The questionnaire was accompanied by a covering letter and a reply-paid envelope. The covering letter reminded the addressee of the original school survey and requested their participation in this survey.

Once again the envelope containing the questionnaire carried a message advising the recipient that it should be forwarded to the person named if he or she had moved. If the current householder did not have a forwarding address they should return the envelope to the sender. Over a period of three months three reminders were sent to those who did not reply within three weeks of any posting. The first reminder consisted of a letter emphasizing the importance of the study while the second and third reminders also contained an extra copy of the questionnaire.

Table 8.1 Sample response rate for each posting

Posting	No. sent	Completed Returns	Blank Returns	Refusals
1st	7543	2817 (37.3%)	702 (9.3%)	7 (0.1%)
2nd	4017	1100 (27.4%)	143 (3.6%)	2 (0.05%)
3rd	2772	613 (22.1%)	241 (8.7%)	19 (0.7%)
4th	1899	248 (13.1%)	67 (3.5%)	4 (0.2%)

Table 8.1 details the response rate to each posting. The blank returns are those questionnaires returned by the Post Office or current householder stating that the person named was not known at that address. The refusals are questionnaires actually returned by the addressee with an indication that they did not wish to participate in the survey. There were very few refusals. This table shows that the response rate declined from 37% for the

first posting to 13% for the fourth posting.

After three reminders 4778 (63.3%) of the targetted sample of 7543 had replied. The declining rate of return to each reminder suggests that a fourth reminder would probably have increased the cumulative response rate to 65% at the most. If the 1153 blank returns are excluded from the orginal sample size on the grounds that these cohort members did not have the opportunity of replying then the overall response rate rises to 74.8% (N=6390).

On receipt, the completed questionnaires were coded for current or previous job and social class using the Registrar General's Classification of Occupations (O.P.C.S., 1981). Cigarette brand preferred was coded using the Government Chemist List. The self-reported tar level of cigarettes was also coded.

The information contained in the questionnaires was then entered onto the computer and the data set prepared was subsequently checked and verified. The data set was then linked to the original 1974-81 Derbyshire data file which contained details of the young people during adolescence.

8.4 Characteristics of the respondents

The respondents to the questionnaire were aged between 21-22 years. Fifty one per cent of those who returned completed questionnaires were female and 49% were male. One third of the women and 17% of the men were married and a small number (3% of the women and 1% of the men) were already separated or divorced. Seventy four per cent of the men were in full-time employment as were 62% of the women. Further details of the marital and employment status of the young people and their smoking behaviour are given in the following chapters.

An estimate of the representativeness of the respondents can be obtained by considering some of the characteristics of those who replied to the different postings. Table 8.2 details the prevalence of smoking of the respondents who replied to each posting and also the cumulative prevalence of smoking.

Table 8.2 Prevalence of smoking among respondents

	Posting Prevalence	(N)	Cumulative Prevalence	(N)
1st Posting	33.1%	(2751)	33.1%	(2751)
2nd Posting	35.1%	(1065)	33.8%	(3816)
3rd Posting	43.7%	(597)	35.1%	(4413)
4th Posting	41.7%	(240)	35.4%	(4653)

This table shows that the prevalence of smoking was higher among those who replied at the fourth posting than among those who replied at the first. This would suggest that the young people who smoked were less likely to reply initially. However, when the cumulative prevalence is considered it is apparent that the prevalence of smoking only increased from 33% to 35% over the four postings. In view of this small increase in the cumulative prevalence it would seem unlikely that the prevalence of smoking among the non-respondents would be much greater than among the respondents overall. This would suggest that the respondents are representative of the cohort, at least in their smoking behaviour.

8.5 Statistical note

The purpose of the next four chapters is to describe the character of the relationship between certain social and psychological variables and the young adults' smoking behaviour.

However, any such relationships which are apparent in the raw data could be due to the influence of other variables. As a guard against this a series of regression analyses were conducted where necessary, with grouped sets of variables controlling for the effect of sex, social class and marital status. In addition, using linked data from the earlier survey the smoking behaviour of the respondents when they were aged 18-19 years was also controlled for in these analyses. Such safeguards mean that any significant relationship which was revealed in the analyses was not due to the hidden effect of these variables.

Estimates greater than two standard errors have been taken as significantly different from zero. This means that the tests are at the 5% level of significance (cf. 1.96). However, it whould be noted that since many such tests were conducted any particular relationship which did reach significance should be considered as no more than a strong indication of an effect.

9 Details of smoking among young adults

9.1 Introduction

This chapter reports the basic details of the smoking behaviour of the young adults surveyed. Most of the questions used to obtain this information had been standardized in previous surveys. Information was also obtained from the ex-smokers on their experience of giving up smoking. Other studies have collected some similar information. The General Household Survey (O.P.C.S., 1985), which is generally regarded as the most representative survey, found that in 1984 the prevalence of smoking among 20-24 year old men was 40% and among women of that age it was 36%. The figures presented in this chapter, besides providing comparative data provide a framework for subsequent analyses which consider the social context of smoking among young adults.

9.2 Prevalence of smoking

Between 1974 and 1978 the prevalence of regular smoking among this cohort of young people rose from 6% of 11-12 year old boys and 2.5% of 11-12 year old girls to 25.9% of 15-16 year old boys and 23.2% of 15-16 girls (Murray et al,1983). In 1981 their responses to a short postal questionnaire revealed that the prevalence of smoking had risen to 33.9% of 18-19 year old boys and 30.5% of 18-19 year old girls.

The prevalence of smoking in 1984 is shown in Table 9.1. This table shows that over 26% of the young men and 19% of the young women were heavy smokers (at least 10 cigarettes a day).

A further 12% of the men and 14% of the women were light smokers (less than 10 cigarettes a day). In addition, 13% of the men and 16% of the women had previously smoked. Thus, roughly half the young men and women were currently smoking or had previously smoked. The steady decline in the rate of increase in the prevalence of smoking during the ten year period of the full study would suggest that it reaches a peak during early adulthood. It is unlikely that many more people start smoking after they reach their mid-twenties.

Table 9.1 Prevalence of smoking

	Male	Female
Non-smoker	48.0%	51.4%
Ex-smoker	13.4%	15.9%
Light smoker (< 10/day)	11.9%	13.6%
Heavy smoker (> 10/day)	26.7%	19.1%
N	2359	2384

9.3 Cigarette consumption patterns

Those young people who described themselves as smokers provided further details of what they smoked and when they smoked. Table 9.2 summarizes the details of the type of tobacco product preferred by both the light and heavy smokers.

Table 9.2 Tobacco product preferred by smokers

	Male		Female	
	Light	Heavy	Light	Heavy
Manufactured cigarettes	69.5%	96.6%	94.7%	98.2%
Hand rolled cigarettes	11.4%	3.4%	4.7%	1.5%
Pipe	3.7%	–	–	0.2%
Cigars	15.4%	–	0.6%	–
N	272	612	320	453

This table shows that the vast majority preferred manufactured cigarettes. However, among the male light smokers over 11% smoked hand rolled cigarettes and a further 15% smoked cigars.

Table 9.3 gives details of the self-reported tar levels of the cigarettes consumed by the smokers. This shows that over half the young people who smoked preferred middle tar cigarettes. Among the men, approximately a quarter smoked low or low to middle tar cigarettes. Almost a fifth of the male light smokers were not aware of the tar level of the cigarettes they smoked. Among the women approximately 40% preferred low or low to middle tar cigarettes. The low tar cigarettes were most popular among the light smokers especially the women. Approximately 2% of the young adults reported that they smoked high tar or middle-to -

113

high tar cigarettes. This small percentage is gratifying in terms of the validity of the responses since such tar levels are no longer available.

Table 9.3 Self-reported tar level of cigarettes smoked

	Male		Female	
	Light	Heavy	Light	Heavy
Low tar	9.3%	5.8%	20.6%	8.9%
Low to middle tar	16.1%	21.5%	21.3%	28.2%
Middle tar	53.7%	69.1%	51.2%	61.1%
Middle to high tar	0.5%	0.7%	1.0%	0.7%
High tar	1.0%	0.2%	1.7%	0.2%
Don't know	19.5%	2.7%	4.1%	0.9%
N	285	585	291	429

Table 9.4 provides details of the tobacco consumption of the smokers in different situations. This table provides a measure of the validity of the initial classification of the young peoples' smoking behaviour. It shows there is a high degree of aggreement between the two measures.

Table 9.4 Tobacco consumption in different situations

	Male		Female	
	Light	Heavy	Light	Heavy
During the day at home or work				
None	41.7%	3.5%	43.4%	1.1%
< 10 cigarettes	45.9%	68.9%	56.4%	74.7%
> 10 cigarettes	3.4%	27.6%	0.3%	24.2%
Pipe/cigars	9.1%	–	–	–
In the evening at home				
None	38.8%	7.9%	41.0%	1.6%
< 10 cigarettes	50.2%	84.3%	58.6%	91.5%
> 10 cigarettes	0.8%	7.9%	0.3%	6.9%
Pipe/cigars	10.1%	–	–	–
In the evening out socially				
None	5.8%	1.2%	4.9%	1.4%
<10 cigarettes	72.9%	61.7%	87.7%	65.0%
>10 cigarettes	6.2%	37.0%	7.1%	33.7%
Pipe/cigars	15.1%	14.1%	1.9%	12.3%
Nmin	237	596	300	440

Over 90% of the heavy smokers smoked in all situations. They were most likely to smoke when out socially and least likely to smoke when at home in the evening. Almost 40% of the light smokers did not smoke at all at work or at home. However, 90% of the light smokers smoked when out socially.

9.4 Smoking career

Table 9.5 details the estimated age when the young people first started smoking regularly. This shows that approximately half the heavy smokers had started smoking regularly before 16 years and another third before they reached 18 years. Among the light smokers over 40% of the men and 30% of the women had started before 16 years and a further 25% of the men and 32% of the women before 18 years. However, over 10% of the heavy smokers and 30% of the light smokers had only started smoking regularly since they reached 18 years. The men began smoking earlier than the women.

Table 9.5 Age started smoking regularly

	Male		Female	
	Light	Heavy	Light	Heavy
12 years	6.8%	6.8%	1.1%	3.6%
12-13 years	8.4%	13.0%	11.6%	10.1%
14-15 years	26.2%	35.1%	18.9%	35.6%
16-17 years	24.9%	34.0%	32.3%	34.0%
18-19 years	21.9%	9.1%	26.6%	14.6%
20+ years	11.8%	2.0%	9.6%	2.1%
N	237	601	285	444

Table 9.6 summarizes the replies of the smokers to a series of questions about giving up smoking. This shows that the majority of smokers would like to give up smoking. This desire was stronger among the heavy than among the light smokers and stronger among the women than among the men. Of those who wanted to give up smoking, health was cited as the most popular reason by the light smokers and cost as the most popular reason by the heavy smokers. Most of the smokers thought that they would feel better if they did manage to stop smoking. This was especially the case among the heavy smokers. Among the young men just over 10% of the light smokers and over 30% of the heavy smokers were concerned that they might gain weight if they stopped smoking. However, over a third of the female light smokers and almost two thirds of the female heavy smokers reported similar concern. These figures would suggest that the light smokers are least concerned about any possible harmful consequences of smoking and have least desire to give up.

This impression is confirmed in Table 9.7. This table details the various attempts the young smokers had made to give up smoking. It shows that the heavy smokers were more likely than the light smokers to have tried to give up. However, they were much more likely to consider it very difficult to give up smoking and less likely in previous attempts to have been without a cigarette for more than a week. The fact that these heavy smokers were more likely to cite cost as a reason for giving up smoking would support the view that price increases would be a particularly potent disincentive to smoking among this group of young adults.

Table 9.6   Reasons for giving up smoking

	Male		Female	
	Light	Heavy	Light	Heavy
Desire to give up smoking				
Definite	54.3%	69.1%	58.8%	74.8%
Do not care	29.7%	20.5%	29.2%	13.6%
Main reasons for giving up				
Cost	31.9%	49.1%	32.6%	52.9%
Health	58.2%	42.3%	55.2%	37.1%
Pregnancy	-	-	6.6%	2.9%
Doctor's advice	-	2.1%	0.6%	2.1%
Media	2.8%	0.9%	0.6%	1.5%
Social pressure	3.5%	3.1%	2.2%	1.8%
Other	3.5%	2.5%	2.2%	1.8%
(N)	(141)	(426)	(181)	(340)
Would feel better after				
giving up	67.2%	86.7%	67.3%	86.8%
Concerned about weight gain				
after giving up	13.2%	31.6%	36.7%	64.9%
Nmin	256	607	301	448

Table 9.7   Attempts to give up smoking

	Male		Female	
	Light	Heavy	Light	Heavy
Attempts to give up				
Never	31.9%	18.8%	28.9%	19.9%
Once	16.3%	24.4%	26.8%	26.6%
More than once	51.7%	56.9%	44.3%	53.5%
Abstinent for a week				
Never	13.4%	18.2%	13.3%	22.7%
1-3 times	60.6%	68.0%	70.2%	67.3%
More than 3 times	27.2%	13.7%	21.4%	9.9%
(N)	(164)	(434)	(173)	(321)
Anticipated difficulty in giving up				
Very difficult	10.6%	40.5%	10.9%	46.8%
Quite difficult	36.6%	50.1%	41.3%	47.5%
Not difficult	52.8%	9.4%	47.8%	5.8%
Nmin	265	607	312	451

Table 9.8 reports how the smokers perceived their smoking behaviour in ten years time. This shows approximately 45% of the light smokers and 40% of the heavy smokers felt that they would not be smoking at all within ten years. A further 32% of the male light smokers and 46% of the female light smokers thought they would only be smoking occasionally then. So too did 14% of the male heavy smokers and 19% of the female heavy smokers. Thus, the majority of the smokers thought they would either give up smoking altogether or reduce their consumption in the following ten years. While this is an optimistic picture it is probable that many of the heavy smokers would experience considerable difficulty in quitting the habit in ten years time.

Table 9.8 Perceived smoking behaviour in 10 years time

	Male		Female	
	Light	Heavy	Light	Heavy
Smoking at least 20 cigarettes daily	3.0%	21.3%	0.6%	18.5%
Smoking less than 20 cigaretes daily	7.4%	23.7%	8.1%	25.6%
Smoking occasionally	31.9%	13.8%	46.1%	19.4%
Smoking a pipe or cigars	13.0%	2.2%	-	0.5%
Not smoking at all	44.8%	39.1%	45.2%	36.1%
N	270	596	310	438

9.6   Ex-smokers

To provide some further information on the process of giving up smoking the ex-smokers were required to answer a series of questions about their previous smoking behaviour and their reasons for giving up. Table 9.10 summarizes their replies.This shows that approximately half the ex-smokers had smoked daily while the rest had smoked occasionally. Approximately three quarters had given up smoking over a year ago and most of the rest at least a month ago. This confirmed that these young people were genuine ex-smokers and had not just stopped smoking recently. The majority of the ex-smokers had not experienced much difficulty in giving up. This contrasts with the heavy smokers and many of the light smokers who anticipated substantial difficulty in giving up.

The most popular reason for giving up was health followed by the cost of smoking. In this respect they were similar to the light smokers whereas more of the heavy smokers thought cost was the main reason for giving up. In addition, 7% of the males and 11% of the females reported social pressure as a reason for giving up. This contrasts with approximately 3% of the smokers who thought that social pressure was a reason for giving up. Finally, over 20% gave an unlisted reason for giving up. Inspection of a proportion of the questionnaires indicated that this was often dislike of the experience of smoking. The ease

with which these young ex-smokers gave up smoking is unlikely to
be the future quitting experience of the heavy smokers. The
majority of the ex-smokers probably did not smoke a lot and not
for a lengthy period. As suggested by the previous section, the
quitting experience of the heavy smoker is more likely to be
protracted and difficult.

Table 9.10 Smoking experience of former smokers

	Male	Female
Frequency of smoking		
Daily	57.0%	49.3%
Occasionally	43.0%	50.7%
Time since last cigarette		
< 1 week	1.0%	0.5%
1 week - 1 month	5.5%	3.2%
1 month - 1 year	20.1%	22.7%
> 1 year	73.4%	72.5%
Difficulty giving up		
Very hard	4.2%	4.2%
Quite hard	19.2%	19.8%
Not hard	75.6%	76.1%
Main reason for stopping		
Cost	26.3%	24.2%
Health	44.1%	34.0%
Pregnant	-	9.2%
Doctors advice	0.3%	0.5%
Media	1.0%	0.8%
Social pressure	6.9%	10.9%
Other	21.4%	20.4%
N	304	363

9.6 Summary

Cigarette smoking is quite a popular activity among over one
third of the young adults surveyed. However, the popularity of
the practice is dependent upon the context, with smoking being
most popular in leisure situations. Many of the smokers did not
smoke at home or at work. Subsequent chapters will consider the
characteristics of each of these situations which are associated
with smoking.

In addition, many of the smokers had only started smoking since
leaving school and most thought that it would not be a life -
long practice. Indeed many had tried to give up smoking,
especially for reasons of cost and health. A substantial number
had given up smoking, especially for health reasons. However,
those currently smoking anticipated considerable difficulty in
giving up.

10 The prevalence of smoking at home

10.1 Introduction

Young people experience substantial change in their living arrangements during early adulthood. This is the period when many of them marry, leave their parents' home and establish a new home with their spouse. Many others organize shared accommodation with friends. Within these new contexts a proportion of the young adults establish a smoking routine. This chapter considers the relationship between smoking at home and the character of the young adults' living arrangements.

In addition, the chapter considers how the young people perceive time at home. The reason for our interest in this issue was that the interview study had suggested that many of the young smokers actively use smoking as a means of exerting personal control over the passage of time. This chapter considers how the perception of time is related to both home situation and smoking behaviour.

To assess how the young adults perceived time at home they were asked to answer Yes or No to a series of questions. These questions were derived from comments made by the sample interviewed. Table 10.1 details the prevalence of smoking at home classified by how the young adults perceived time there. It should be noted that those who did not smoke at home were classified as non-smokers. A regression analysis found that those young adults who "often felt that time drags" or that they "often wasted their time" at home were significantly more likely to smoke. Subsequent sections will consider not only the extent to which smoking varied across home situations but also to what extent these two variables also varied across some of these situations.

119

Table 10.1 Prevalence of smoking at home classified by
perception of time at home

		Male (n)	Female (n)
"Do you usually know what	Yes	27.4% (1399)	24.1% (1243)
time it is?"	No	32.6% (904)	27.0% (1122)
"Do you usually care what	Yes	25.5% (877)	25.9% (1108)
time it is?"	No	31.9% (1426)	24.8% (1252)
"Do you often feel that	Yes	40.9% (660)	38.4% (735)
time drags?"	No	24.6% (1615)	19.6% (1604)
"Do you feel you often	Yes	35.1% (1154)	29.5% (1128)
waste your time?"	No	23.3% (1134)	21.4% (1219)
"Are you often surprised	Yes	26.9% (1521)	24.5% (1795)
how quickly time has passed?"	No	34.8% (778)	28.0% (557)

10.2 Marital status

Among the 2389 young women 60.6% were single, 32.9% were
married, a further 2.9% were separated or divorced while the
remainder classified themselves as 'other' and were probably co-
habiting. Among the 2329 young men 79.0% were unmarried, 16.6%
were married, a further 1.3% were already separated or divorced
and the remaining 3.5% were 'other'. Thus the women were almost
exactly twice as likely as the men to be married, or separated,
at this age.

Table 10.2 details the prevalence of smoking at home classified
according to their marital status. The prevalence was lowest
among those who were still unmarried and highest among the small
group who were separated or divorced. Among the men, those who
were married were significantly more likely to smoke than their
unmarried peers. A similar relationship was not apparent among
the young women.

Table 10.2 Prevalence of smoking at home classified by
marital status

	Male (n)	Female (n)
Single	26.7% (1851)	24.4% (1468)
Married	37.4% (390)	25.5% (797)
Separated/Divorced	66.7% (30)	48.6% (70)
Other	48.3% (58)	29.6% (54)

Table 10.3 cross-tabulates with marital status the proportion
of young people who felt that time dragged or that they wasted
time at home. This shows that the young people who had
separated were significantly more likely to think that time drags
at home. In addition, the young men who had separated were
significantly more likely to think that they wasted their time at
home.

**Table 10.3   Perception of time at home classified by marital
status**

	Nmin	Time Drags	Waste Time
Male			
Single	1802	30.7%	52.4%
Married	374	18.9%	39.3%
Separated	28	53.6%	72.4%
Other	58	24.1%	48.3%
Female			
Single	1426	31.3%	54.1%
Married	770	29.6%	37.1%
Separated	67	58.2%	50.7%
Other	51	27.5%	48.1%

After the turmoil of making and breaking a relationship at such
an early age homelife for the young people who were separated was
probably rather quiet. It is within this context that the value
of smoking increases. The cigarette could almost be considered a
substitute companion for the missing spouse.

It was noticeable that the single men and women were more
likely than those who were married to think that time drags at
home. However, they were less likely than them to smoke. A
possible reason for this is that many of the single people lived
with their parents who may discourage smoking at home.This was
mentioned by several of the young people interviewed (see Section
3.9). The importance of this factor is apparent in the following
section.

10.3 Living arrangements

The living arrangements of the young people were related to
their marital status. Among those who were unmarried the vast
majority still lived with their parents. Table 10.4 shows that
smoking was least prevalent among these young people. Among the
young men smoking was most prevalent among those who lived alone.
Smoking was also quite high among the young women who lived
alone. These young people are removed from any possible parental
restrictions against smoking. Among the young women smoking was
highest among those who lived with a single parent. In previous
research (Murray et al, 1985) adolescents from single parent
families were more likely to smoke. It may be that for this group
of young women smoking is a means of handling the conflict

between responsibility for a single parent and desire to develop an independent life.

Table 10.4 Prevalence of smoking at home classified by
              living arrangements

	Male (n)	Female (n)

Single

With both parents	24.7% (1188)	18.5% (820)
With one parent	29.1% (213)	38.1% (155)
With friends	29.8% (171)	27.0% (196)
Alone	35.3% (85)	30.0% (100)
Other	29.9% (177)	30.2% (172)

Married

| With spouse | 37.7% (363) | 24.8% (759) |
| Other | 28.0% (25) | 36.1% (36) |

Table 10.5 cross-tabulates with living arrangements how the young single people perceived time at home. This shows that the men who lived alone and the women who lived with a single parent were more likely to think that they were wasting their time at home. For whatever reason this occurred smoking seemed to be a means of coping with this frustration.

Table 10.5 Perception of time at home classified by living
              arrangements of single people

	Nmin	Time Drags	Waste Time

Male

With both parents	1162	29.6%	51.0%
With one parent	201	39.3%	55.7%
With friends	168	28.6%	50.9%
Alone	83	25.3%	59.5%
Other	188	33.0%	56.1%

Female

With both parents	800	31.1%	54.2%
With one parent	149	36.0%	59.7%
With friends	193	22.8%	54.4%
Alone	95	40.2%	56.7%
Other	184	32.8%	47.8%

10.4 Smoking behaviour of parents and spouse

Parental smoking is an important influence on the development of smoking among adolescents (Murray et al, 1983). This was confirmed in many of the comments the young people made in the interviews when discussing their early experience of smoking (see section 3.7). Table 10.6 indicates that such a relationship is maintained into adulthood.

Table 10.6 Prevalence of smoking at home classified by parental smoking

	Male (n)	Female (n)
Mother		
No mother	37.8% (82)	32.6% (92)
Non-smoker	34.9% (1311)	27.6% (1414)
Occasional smoker	47.9% (188)	41.3% (150)
Regular smoker	39.6% (688)	38.7% (691)
Father		
No father	39.3% (155)	37.5% (168)
Non-smoker	33.6% (1017)	27.2% (1057)
Occasional smoker	37.2% (129)	38.7% (111)
Regular smoker	43.1% (755)	36.0% (754)
Pipe/Cigar smoker	34.3% (204)	30.8% (243)

Those young people whose father smoked were significantly more likely to smoke themselves. A similar relationship with mothers approached but failed to reach significance. There was, however, a suggestion that regular smoking among mothers was somewhat less likely than occasional smoking to be associated with smoking among the young adults. This would agree with some of the comments made by some of the non-smokers that their parents' smoking had acted as a disincentive to them adopting smoking (see section 3.7).

The relationship between spouses' smoking practices was also considered. Table 10.7 shows that those young people whose spouse smoked were significantly more likely to smoke themselves.

Table 10.7 Prevalence of smoking at home classified by spouse's smoking

	Male (n)	Female (n)
Non-smoker	26.1% (257)	11.2% (437)
Occasional smoker	50.0% (28)	38.2% (55)
Regular smoker	66.3% (92)	51.2% (248)
Pipe/Cigar smoker	-	6.9% (29)

In the interviews (see Section 6.3) many of the young people had mentioned that whether someone smoked was a factor in deciding whether they went out with that person. This form of assortative mating seems to have continued into marriage.

10.5 Evening activities

As an indication of what they did at home in the evening the young people were required to answer how often they watched television, did housework, or did nothing special. Table 10.8 details the prevalence of smoking at home classified by evening activities and by marital status. Watching television was most popular among those who were married: over two thirds of them watched it most evenings. It was less popular among the young single women, 40.0% of whom watched it most evenings, and least popular among the young single men of whom only 33.2% watched it most evenings. This largely agrees with the interviews (see Section 3.6) where many of the young single men reported their eagerness to get out of the house in the evenings. Only among the married men was smoking more prevalent among those who watched television most evenings. Perhaps these men have little role in household activities. Instead they while away the evening smoking in front of the television.

Table 10.8 Prevalence of smoking at home classified by evening activities and marital status

| | Single | | Married | |
	Male (n)	Female (n)	Male (n)	Female (n)
Watch television				
Most evenings	29.0%(606)	26.5%(585)	42.2%(256)	25.8%(543)
Some evenings	25.0%(1151)	22.5%(827)	26.4%(129)	24.9%(237)
Never	26.1%(69)	22.0%(41)	- (2)	- (9)
Do housework				
Most evenings	32.5%(40)	31.5%(130)	38.1%(21)	27.9%(301)
Some evenings	27.8%(510)	24.2%(829)	39.2%(222)	24.3%(420)
Never	25.6%(1209)	22.8%(465)	32.8%(134)	16.7%(60)
Do nothing				
Most evenings	35.3%(184)	33.0%(182)	48.3%(60)	23.5%(149)
Some evenings	25.6%(937)	22.9%(813)	34.6%(179)	23.7%(409)
Never	23.8%(509)	23.1%(281)	31.6%(95)	25.6%(125)

Not surprisingly, it was the married women who did housework most frequently. The men, both married and unmarried, were least likely to do housework. In all groups those who did housework frequently were more likely to smoke. For these young people housework was almost a job and like Dennis (Section 3.5), who used smoking to organize his work routine, smoking was possibly used as a means of marking out the breaks between one household task and the next.

The married women were most likely and the unmarried men least likely to think that they did nothing in the evenings. By this they probably meant that they did not involve themselves in social activities outside the home. The single men and women and the married men who did nothing most evenings were more likely to smoke. The single men and women probably felt frustrated sitting around the house 'doing nothing'. Since they were less likely to have family and household responsibilities time would pass slowly. Smoking would be a means of passing the time. The married men who had not yet identified a role for themselves around the house probably experienced similar feelings and would experience a similar value in smoking.

10.6 Reasons for smoking at home

According to Tomkins' (1966) classification of smoking motivation there are six main reasons for smoking: stimulation, sensorinator manipulation, pleasurable relaxation, negative affect, addiction and habit. All of the young people who smoked were asked whether or not they smoked for these reasons at home. In addition, they were asked the importance of "boredom" and "nothing to do" as reasons for smoking at home. Table 10.9 summarizes their replies.

Table 10.9 Reasons for smoking at home

| | Single | | Married | |
	Male	Female	Male	Female
Stimulation	3.8%	3.2%	0.7%	5.7%
Manipulation	23.6%	24.7%	24.8%	25.9%
Relaxation	83.5%	79.2%	85.0%	81.8%
Negative affect	70.4%	88.4%	76.8%	93.9%
Addiction	56.9%	52.0%	69.1%	62.2%
Habit	32.4%	33.4%	40.0%	52.8%
"Boredom"	73.1%	77.1%	73.2%	82.2%
"Nothing to do"	64.0%	70.4%	68.3%	80.3%
Nmin	475	342	136	185

This shows that, in general, the most popular reasons were 'relaxation', 'negative affect' and 'boredom'. The women were more likely than the men to claim that they smoked when upset or when they had nothing to do at home. Those who were married were more likely than the single people to smoke when they were upset or had nothing to do at home. They were also more likely to give addiction or habit as reasons for smoking at home. Thus smoking was seen by many of the smokers as an aid to relaxation. In the minds of many of them it was probably associated with the period after a meal or while watching television. It was one of their home comforts.

In addition, it seemed to be frequently used as a means of coping with the various conflicts at home. This was especially apparent among the married women who were least likely to enjoy the opportunity of social relations outside the home. The young single men were least likely to list negative affect as a reason for smoking. They were most likely to spend time outside the home where they could enjoy a variety of social experiences. Often alone at home the young married woman seemd especially prone to use smoking as a means of coping with negative emotional experiences.

Finally, smoking was also seen by many of the young adults as a means of coping with boredom at home. This would confirm our previous analyses (see Table 10.1) which showed that those who thought that time dragged at home were more likely to smoke there.

10.7 Smoking at home among the unemployed and housewives

The overall prevalence figures showed that smoking was particularly popular among both the unemployed and housewives. The interview study suggested that a possible reason for this was the lack of routine in the lives of the unemployed and housewives (see Sections 3.11 and 3.13). To investigate this possible relationship further the young people without a job outside the home were required to answer a series of questions about their daily routine: how long was it since they held a job, their daytime activities, their companions and the extent to which they planned their day. Table 10.10 details the prevalence of smoking at home among the unemployed and housewives classified according to their responses to these questions.

Table 10.10 Prevalence of smoking at home among unemployed and housewives

	Male Unemployed(n)	Female Unemployed(n)	Housewives (n)
Time since last job			
< 6 months	57.7% (71)	39.6% (46)	21.4%(28)
6-12 months	38.3% (60)	35.3% (34)	30.6%(49)
> 12 months	44.8% (125)	41.3% (80)	35.5%(256)
Usual daytime companions			
Spouse	55.6% (81)	54.8% (31)	29.7%(128)
Close friend	50.0% (54)	33.3% (27)	55.6%(36)
Lots of friends	29.4% (17)	28.6% (7)	50.0%(2)
Family	40.4% (57)	37.8% (74)	27.9%(136)
No one	37.5% (40)	30.4% (23)	44.0%(25)
Extent to which day planned			
Usually	42.1% (38)	29.6% (27)	34.7%(75)
Sometimes	44.4% (160)	37.5% (109)	30.0%(210)
Never	56.3% (64)	46.9% (32)	45.9%(61)

Among the unemployed there was no direct relationship between period of unemployment and extent of smoking at home. However, those women who had been housewives for more than a year were more likely than other housewives to be smokers. This is probably a reflexion of the fact that those who marry early tend to be smokers.

126

Among the unemployed and housewives the most frequent daytime companion was spouse or family. The unemployed whose usual daytime companion was their spouse were most likely to smoke. Sitting at home most of the day, perhaps sharing a cigarette with a spouse was a means of shared coping with the hardships of unemployment such as social isolation and boredom. It recalls the comment of Carl (Section 3.11) who felt that for his wife and himself smoking was one of the few comforts left in a very harried life.

It was interesting to note that among the unemployed the prevalence of smoking was lowest among the small proportion who had lots of friends. These young people had somehow managed to evade some of the social and psychological consequences of unemployment. However, this was a small group of people and not typical of the lot of most of the unemployed.

The housewives whose usual daytime companion was a close friend were more likely to smoke than other housewives. Graham (1976) has described the social value of smoking to married women. According to her it is a time "when the harassed mother can temporarily escape from the exactions of full time motherhood. During such interludes, the children are expected to entertain themselves, for the mother is not oriented to them but to herself or to her peer group". Sharing a cigarette with a friend thus emerges as a coping device for some mothers.

Finally, Table 10.10 shows that most of the young people, in particular the women, planned their days to some extent. Among the small proportion who did not plan their days smoking was more prevalent. These are the young people, like Jason (Section 3.13), who would sit around the house all day. Smoking was a means of passing the time for them.

The housewives were most likely to plan their days. This was a consequence of their household and family responsibilities. Table 10.11 details the prevalence of smoking at home classified according to the nature of the daytime activities of the unemployed and housewives. It shows almost all the housewives did housework most days compared with two thirds of the unemployed women and less than one quarter of the unemployed men. Smoking was more prevalent among those unemployed who did housework regularly. Again, as for housework in the evenings, regular housework during the day has many of the characteristics of a full time job. Smoking can be of value to some people as a means of organizing this work routine. The housewives were also more likely than the unemployed to go shopping frequently and to look after children. Among all groups, but especially among the unemployed men smoking was more prevalent among those with responsibilities for children. It may be, as has been suggested by Graham (1976), that for those people frequently involved in childcare smoking is a means of reaffirming adult status. She suggested that "smoking provides both a sense of body autonomy and role distance, a time when children are forbidden to climb on mother's knee and to demand attention". Those who frequently visited friends were also more likely to smoke. This again was an opportunity for reaffirming adult status through conversation and the exchange of cigarettes.

Table 10.11 Prevalence of smoking at home classified by
frequency of daytime activities

	Unemployed		
	Male (n)	Female (n)	Housewives (n)
Housework			
Most days	55.2% (58)	45.4% (110)	35.1% (333)
Some days	46.5% (127)	25.5% (55)	- (12)
Never	46.5% (56)	- (1)	- (0)
Shopping			
Most days	50.0% (32)	45.8% (59)	36.7% (139)
Some days	43.6% (102)	34.3% (102)	32.8% (204)
Never	63.8% (47)	40.0% (5)	- (1)
Childcare			
Most days	58.8% (17)	63.4% (41)	35.0% (286)
Some days	70.6% (34)	28.0% (25)	30.8% (13)
Never	44.6% (177)	31.8% (86)	26.3% (38)
Visiting			
Most days	46.2% (65)	51.1% (45)	34.9% (86)
Some days	50.3% (161)	36.4% (110)	33.3% (252)
Never	30.0% (20)	12.5% (8)	- (2)
Nothing			
Most days	45.2% (84)	31.4% (35)	34.8% (66)
Some days	54.3% (116)	46.3% (82)	35.6% (174)
Never	41.2% (34)	28.6% (21)	22.8% (57)

10.8 Summary

The prevalence of smoking was clearly related to a variety of
the characteristics of the young adults' home situation.
Considering marital status, it emerged that the small group who
were separated or divorced were most likely to smoke. Since time
particularly dragged at home for these young adults it was
suggested that smoking was valuable to them at home almost as a
substitute companion for the missing spouse.

Smoking was also more prevalent among the young men who lived
alone and among the young women who lived with a single parent.
They often felt that they wasted their time at home. It was
suggested that smoking was used by these young people as a means
of coping with the frustration of what they felt was wasted time.

Smoking among the young adults was clearly related to that of
their parents indicating the important role they play as a model,
especially during adolescence (cf. Murray et al, 1984). In
addition, the strong relationship between the smoking behaviour
of spouses suggests the operation of a form of assortative mating
in the selection of a partner.

The popularity of smoking was also related to the young adults' involvement in certain evening activities. In addition, among the unemployed and housewives smoking at home was related to the character of their daily home routine. Those who did not have an organized daily routine were most likely to smoke. The unemployed men found it most difficult to plan their days at home. Since they were largely excluded from household tasks their days passed very slowly at home. Smoking was valuable when considered within this context.

11 The prevalence of smoking at work

11.1 Introduction

The majority of the young men and women surveyed worked full-time outside the home. According to their own reports (see Table 9.5) a substantial proportion of them smoked while at work. The interview study suggested that smoking was closely integrated into the working routine of many of the young adults. This chapter considers the character of the relationship between smoking at work and a variety of working conditions. Once again, how the young adults perceived time is considered an intermediary mechanism between social situation and smoking.

Table 11.1 Prevalence of smoking at work classified by perception of time at work

		Male (n)	Female (n)
"Do you usually know	Yes	28.8% (1374)	23.8% (1325)
what time it is?"	No	34.2% (851)	27.5% (826)
"Do you usually care	Yes	29.1% (1627)	23.8% (1726)
what time it is?"	No	35.7% (596)	30.8% (416)
"Do you often feel	Yes	35.1% (1178)	27.6% (1169)
that time drags?"	No	25.9% (1022)	22.5% (939)
"Do you often feel	Yes	35.4% (616)	28.5% (478)
you waste your time?"	No	29.0% (1590)	23.9% (1643)
"Are you often	Yes	30.4% (1542)	25.0% (1578)
surprised at how	No	32.0% (682)	25.0% (563)
quickly time has passed?"			

In the same way as the young adults answered a series of questions about how they perceived time at home, they also answered a series of questions about how they perceived time at work. Table 11.1 details the prevalence of smoking at work classified by how they perceived time there. A regression analysis which controlled for the effects of marital status and social class considered the relationship between the time variables and smoking at work. This found that the young adults who usually "knew the time" and "cared about the time" at work were significantly less likely to smoke while those who felt that "time dragged" at work were significantly more likely to smoke. Where appropriate, the relationship between these time variables and the work situation is considered in the following sections.

11.2 Work status and social class

Table 11.2 summarizes the overall prevalence of smoking among the young adults classified by their work status. Among the young men smoking was most prevalent among the unemployed, followed by those with a part-time job and then by those who had a full-time job or were in the forces. Among the young women, smoking was again most prevalent among the unemployed, followed by the housewives and the small number who were in the forces. Smoking was least prevalent among those women with a job, either full-time or part-time. For both sexes, the prevalence of smoking was low amongst those whose work status was classified as 'other'. Review of a sample of the questionnaires indicated that many of these respondents were students.

Table 11.2 Prevalence of smoking classified by work status

	(n)	Non-Smoker	Light Smoker	Heavy Smoker
Full-time job				
Male	(1692)	62.9%	11.1%	25.9%
Female	(1461)	70.9%	13.8%	15.3%
Part-time job				
Male	(39)	48.8%	20.5%	30.8%
Female	(100)	68.0%	6.0%	26.0%
Housewife	(343)	61.8%	9.9%	28.3%
Housewife/ part-time job	(48)	58.4%	10.4%	31.3%
Unemployed				
Male	(261)	45.2%	11.5%	43.3%
Female	(167)	52.1%	18.6%	29.3%
Forces				
Male	(73)	65.8%	9.6%	24.7%
Female	(19)	57.9%	15.8%	26.3%
Other/Unknown				
Male	(223)	70.0%	17.5%	12.6%
Female	(233)	65.2%	17.6%	17.2%

Table 11.3 details the prevalence of smoking among those with a job classified by the Registrar General's (O.P.C.S., 1981) categorization of these jobs. In this and subsequent chapters the Registrar General's classification of occupations is used as a measure of social class and, in particular, to classify the workers as either manual or non-manual. Table 11.3 shows a clear relationship between social class and the prevalence of smoking with smoking being much more prevalent among those with a manual job. In addition, among those who smoked, those with a manual job were more likely to smoke at work. Subsequent sections consider in more detail the relationship between the character of manual and non-manual jobs and smoking at work.

Table 11.3 Smoking practice according to social class among the employed

Social Class	Sex	N	Smoke at work	Smoke elsewhere	Do Not smoke
I	Male	42	14.3%	11.9%	73.8%
Professional	Female	18	-	5.6%	94.4%
II	Male	144	16.0%	6.3%	77.8%
Intermediate	Female	232	19.4%	5.6%	75.0%
III N	Male	224	22.3%	4.9%	72.8%
Skilled non-manual	Female	722	17.0%	6.0%	77.0%
III M	Male	795	31.1%	5.4%	63.5%
Skilled manual	Female	185	22.2%	4.9%	73.0%
IV	Male	364	34.6%	4.7%	60.7%
Partly skilled	Female	275	33.1%	6.5%	60.4%
V	Male	97	44.3%	1.0%	54.6%
Unskilled	Female	20	45.0%	-	55.0%
Other	Male	35	31.4%	8.6%	60.0%
	Female	33	33.3%	6.1%	60.6%

11.3 Job structure

To provide an overview of how the young people's jobs were structured those who worked were required to give a Yes or No reply to four questions:

"Do you work shifts?"

"Are you required to clock on?"

"Do you work overtime regularly?"

"Are you paid piece-rate?"

Table 11.4 details the prevalence of smoking at work classified according to their replies to these questions. This shows that among all the young adults those who worked shiftwork were more likely to smoke. However, this relationship did not reach significance in the regression analysis. Among the non-manual workers those who had to clock on were significantly less likely to smoke at work. This practice is perhaps an indicator of a more structured office routine in which there is less opprtunity for smoking. In addition, the small number of non-manual males who worked piece-rate were significantly more likely to smoke. It may be that for these workers piece-rate is an indicator of a particularly harrowing environment which is relieved by smoking. When time was considered as a possible intermediary variable a comparable relationship between these particular work characteristics and whether or not the workers usually knew the time at work was apparent.

Table 11.4 Prevalence of smoking at work classified by work organisation

		Non-manual		Manual	
		Male (n)	Female (n)	Male (n)	Female (n)
Shiftwork	Yes	23.9% (46)	25.3% (166)	40.1% (379)	33.3% (66)
	No	18.8% (361)	15.5% (802)	30.0% (870)	28.2% (411)
Clock-on	Yes	11.9% (59)	13.2% (129)	33.8% (717)	33.2% (286)
	No	20.6% (349)	17.8% (838)	32.3% (523)	22.9% (192)
Over-time	Yes	19.3% (140)	20.4% (137)	34.2% (530)	31.9% (116)
	No	19.2% (266)	16.5% (826)	32.3% (716)	27.9% (358)
Piece-rate	Yes	28.6% (14)	18.2% (22)	31.4% (172)	29.6% (189)
	No	19.1% (392)	17.1% (925)	33.3% (1053)	28.7% (286)

Table 11.5 details the proportion of young adults who reported that they usually knew the time at work. Generally these young workers were less likely to smoke (see Table 11.1). This table shows that those who worked shifts were less likely to know the time at work. Since these workers were also more likely to smoke, it is possible that smoking was used by them as a means of bringing structure to this apparently disorienting time schedule.

The non-manual workers who clocked on were more likely to know the time. Since they were less likely to smoke, it may be that smoking was of less value to them as a means of structuring time since there was such clear regulation of their working day. Conversely, the female manual workers who clocked on were less likely to know the time. However, they were more likely to smoke. Female manual jobs tend to be particularly routine (see Section 4.4). The occasion of smoking would provide a welcome release from the endless hours of drudgery endured by them at work. It could also provide them with an opportunity for interaction with their workmates which, as many of them indicated (see Section 4.6), was the most important component of their work.

133

Table 11.5 Proportion who usually know the time at work classified by work organisation

		Non-manual Male (n)	Female (n)	Manual Male (n)	Female (n)
Shiftwork	Yes	60.9% (46)	56.0% (166)	53.6% (379)	58.5% (65)
	No	66.7% (366)	63.0% (797)	63.2% (869)	69.4% (415)
Clock-on	Yes	77.6% (58)	69.5% (128)	61.3% (715)	66.6% (287)
	No	64.5% (355)	60.6% (834)	59.2% (525)	69.9% (193)
Overtime	Yes	69.7% (142)	57.2% (138)	63.2% (530)	60.3% (116)
	No	64.3% (269)	62.6% (821)	58.0% (715)	70.6% (361)
Piece-rate	Yes	92.3% (13)	82.6% (23)	60.8% (171)	76.4% (191)
	No	65.3% (398)	61.4% (919)	60.3% (1055)	62.0% (287)

Similarly, the women workers who worked overtime were less likely to know the time at work and more likely to smoke while there. As with clocking-on, overtime is probably indicative of a particularly tedious job which was relieved by smoking.

11.4 Break arrangements

One particular aspect of work organization considered in more detail was the opportunity the young people had to take breaks at work. The interview study had suggested that the character of the break system at work was related to the prevalence of smoking there (see Section 4.5). In this survey the young people were requested to give a Yes or No reply to four questions about their breaks:

"Do you have 'official' breaks which allow you to stop work for short periods of time (apart from meal breaks)?"

"Do you take breaks other than official breaks?"

"Is there a special place for you to go to during breaktimes, i.e. are you able to leave your job?"

"Do you usually spend your break talking to workmates?"

Table 11.6 reports the prevalence of smoking at work classified by the character of the break arrangements. In the regression analysis it emerged that those who had unofficial breaks or had a place to have their breaks were significantly more likely to smoke. In addition, the young women who had official breaks were significantly more likely to smoke. Thus, for many of the young adults it would seem that breaks provided an opportunity for smoking.

The young adults probably took unofficial breaks for a variety of reasons. Table 11.7 considers whether or not how they perceived time at work was related to their taking unofficial

Table 11.6 Prevalence of smoking at work classified by break arrangements

	Non-manual		Manual	
	Male (n)	Female (n)	Male (n)	Female (n)
Official breaks				
Yes	17.9% (145)	19.3% (404)	32.3% (643)	31.9%(288)
No	19.9% (261)	15.6% (564)	34.0% (597)	24.7%(186)
Unofficial breaks				
Yes	18.1% (182)	20.6% (277)	37.4% (650)	40.4%(141)
No	20.0% (225)	15.8% (684)	28.9% (592)	24.3%(329)
Break place				
Yes	18.4% (223)	18.6% (583)	35.6% (769)	29.6%(389)
No	20.7% (179)	15.0% (373)	28.9% (471)	27.1%(85)
Break with mates				
Yes	18.1% (282)	17.7% (733)	33.6%(1036)	29.3%(417)
No	20.9% (115)	16.0% (213)	30.8%(195)	26.9%(52)

breaks there. It shows that those who thought that time dragged at work were more likely to take unofficial breaks.

Table 11.7 Proportion taking unofficial breaks

		Non-manual		Manual	
		Male (n)	Female (n)	Male (n)	Female (n)
Time drags	Yes	50.0%(154)	30.8%(465)	53.8%(738)	30.0%(317)
	No	40.8%(255)	26.6%(473)	50.1%(493)	29.9%(147)

11.5 Smoking arrangements

Table 11.8 considers the relationship between particular arrangements for smoking at work and the prevalence of smoking there. It shows that smoking was more prevalent in those workplaces where cigarettes were on sale and where other workers also smoked. The latter relationship reached significance in a regression analysis. This reaffirms the importance of the normative factor in the maintenance of smoking at work.

In addition, smoking was more prevalent in those workplaces where smoking was restricted to breaks. Calculation of the distribution of such workplaces shows that 14.5% of the non-manual males, 27.2% of the non-manual females, 11.2% of the manual males and 38.6% of the manual females were only allowed to smoke during breaks. Restricted from smoking while working, many of the young workers seem to more than compensate for this during breaks. Indeed, as was the case in the factory where Barry worked (see Section 4.5), for many workers to have a break means to have a cigarette and vice versa.

Table 11.8 Prevalence of smoking at work classified by smoking arrangements

		Non-manual		Manual	
		Male (n)	Female (n)	Male (n)	Female (n)
Cigarettes sold	Yes	20.1%(174)	20.1%(369)	37.7%(544)	32.0%(206)
at work	No	19.1%(230)	15.9%(580)	30.2%(692)	27.9%(258)
Smoking	Yes	20.0%(210)	14.6%(391)	31.4%(563)	26.0%(73)
allowed	Restricted	16.7%(120)	18.4%(245)	35.1%(308)	31.5%(178)
at work	In breaks	27.1%(59)	22.3%(260)	36.0%(139)	32.0%(181)
	No	5.6%(18)	11.5%(61)	34.4%(227)	18.9%(37)
Workmates	All	33.3%(30)	32.8%(364)	46.3%(242)	40.1%(90)
smoke	Some	21.2%(165)	21.4%(392)	36.4%(566)	33.1%(245)
	None	14.4%(209)	12.5%(504)	22.2%(428)	17.3%(133)

11.6 Social relations at work

In the interview study it emerged that for many of the young adults the most important aspect of their work was the character of their relations with their workmates. To assess the relationship between social relations at work and smoking behaviour there, the questionnaire asked a series of questions about the young adults' social relations at work. Table 11.9 details the prevalence of smoking classified by the young adults' replies to these questions about their workmates.

Table 11.9 Prevalence of smoking at work classified by details of social relations

		Non-manual		Manual	
		Male (n)	Female (n)	Male (n)	Female (n)
Works alone	Yes	21.7%(143)	15.4%(247)	28.7%(436)	25.9%(108)
	No	18.0%(266)	17.7%(716)	35.8%(800)	30.1%(366)
Workmates same	Yes	18.6%(237)	17.2%(650)	32.3%(1138)	30.1%(408)
sex	No	20.0%(165)	17.2%(309)	41.4%(111)	25.8%(62)
Gets on with	Yes	18.6%(382)	16.8%(920)	33.5%(1186)	29.9%(445)
older workers	No	17.6%(17)	19.0%(42)	25.0%(52)	20.0%(20)
Socialize with	Most	42.9%(21)	14.8%(54)	47.6%(82)	27.6%(29)
workmates	Some	17.9%(252)	18.3%(606)	34.6%(811)	31.7%(290)
	None	17.2%(128)	16.0%(306)	26.5%(359)	26.3%(152)

Among the manual workers those who worked alone were less likely to smoke whereas among the non-manual workers there was no apparent relationship. Evidence from the interview study (see Section 4.6) suggested that manual workers place greater emphasis on the value of social relations at work. Isolated from workmates they would thus be least likely to experience a social need for smoking at work. This was the case with Ken and Terry (see Section 4.6) who did not smoke.

Both male and female manual workers were more likely to smoke if their workmates were women. Among non-manual workers there was no clear relationship. This would suggest that female company in the manual workplace is more conducive to smoking. In the case of all-female company this would agree with the comments of the women in the interviews (see Section 4.6) that smoking was an important facilitator and regulator of social interaction in the manual workplace. The interview study did not provide details of the experience of male manual workers working mostly with women. The survey indicates that smoking is more prevalent among this minority of men. Perhaps they smoke as a means of maintaining a sense of distance between themselves and the women.

The manual workers were more likely to smoke if they enjoyed good social relations with older workers. There was no such relationship among non-manual workers. This would suggest that age differences are of more importance in the establishment of social relations in the manual workplace. Difficult social relations with older workers is probably indicative of an awkard work situation which is less conducive to smoking.

Finally, the men who socialized with their workmates after work were more likely to smoke than other men. This relationship was not apparent among the women. This question about after work social relations was used as a measure of the intensity of social relations with workmates. There was no sex or social class difference in the reply to this question indicating that the majority of the young adults enjoyed strong social relations with their workmates. The relationship with smoking would suggest that smoking has a more important role to play in the maintenance of strong social relations among men than among women.

11.7 Intrinsic job characteristics

Much of the discussion on work in the interview study revolved around concepts such as variety, responsibility and boredom (see Section 4.4). In their extensive investigations of the psychological characteristics of work Warr, Cook and Wall (1979) classified a series of rather similar constructs which they considered influential in explaining satisfaction with work. They termed these constructs intrinsic job characteristics. In a previous study of smoking among nurses (Murray, Swan and Mattar, 1983) it was found that there was a relationship between the presence of some of these intrinsic job characteristics and smoking. This survey also considered the character of these relationships.

In the questionnaire, those young adults who worked were required to identify along a five-point scale ranging from "There's none of that in my work" to "There's a great deal of that in my work", the extent of presence of seven intrinsic job characteristics in their work. Table 11.10 summarizes the prevalence of smoking at work among the young people classified by the degree of presence of the various intrinsic job characteristics. The degree of presence has been grouped into 'little' (none, little), 'moderate' amount, and 'lots' (quite a lot, lots). It was noticeable that the manual workers, especially the women, reported the least presence of any intrinsic job characteristic.

Table 11.10 Prevalence of smoking at work classified by presence of intrinsic job characteristics

	Non-manual				Manual			
	Male	(n)	Female	(n)	Male	(n)	Female	(n)
Variety								
Little	27.0%	(37)	21.4%	(117)	39.7%	(262)	32.3%	(158)
Moderate	12.1%	(99)	14.7%	(252)	28.7%	(300)	29.9%	(158)
Lots	20.8%	(269)	17.7%	(577)	31.7%	(649)	26.1%	(176)
Responsibility								
Little	10.8%	(37)	16.8%	(149)	40.8%	(206)	32.3%	(158)
Moderate	17.6%	(85)	15.9%	(214)	32.7%	(321)	26.4%	(121)
Lots	20.8%	(283)	18.0%	(583)	30.2%	(685)	28.2%	(188)
Freedom to choose								
Little	20.8%	(72)	14.2%	(219)	39.1%	(253)	25.6%	(195)
Moderate	15.3%	(98)	16.5%	(273)	32.8%	(296)	29.7%	(111)
Lots	20.5%	(234)	19.8%	(449)	30.4%	(654)	34.4%	(160)
Promotion prospects								
Little	17.1%	(105)	20.6%	(399)	32.9%	(680)	29.8%	(349)
Moderate	13.6%	(110)	16.0%	(263)	32.0%	(300)	28.1%	(64)
Lots	24.0%	(183)	14.6%	(281)	33.0%	(221)	27.7%	(47)
Skill usage								
Little	18.4%	(76)	16.1%	(217)	37.4%	(326)	30.8%	(211)
Moderate	14.3%	(84)	15.4%	(240)	30.1%	(289)	25.0%	(100)
Lots	21.2%	(245)	19.1%	(487)	30.8%	(585)	30.9%	(149)
Recognition given								
Little	16.0%	(106)	15.9%	(233)	34.1%	(505)	29.1%	(196)
Moderate	16.5%	(109)	14.2%	(267)	32.0%	(300)	26.0%	(123)
Lots	22.2%	(189)	20.0%	(444)	31.1%	(399)	31.3%	(144)
Attention paid								
Little	20.4%	(108)	15.1%	(251)	33.8%	(456)	28.6%	(248)
Moderate	15.2%	(112)	13.6%	(295)	31.5%	(333)	28.7%	(101)
Lots	21.4%	(182)	21.2%	(397)	32.1%	(405)	31.5%	(111)
Overall								
Little	22.2%	(18)	15.1%	(74)	40.3%	(288)	28.4%	(194)
Moderate	15.9%	(88)	17.1%	(245)	30.0%	(450)	28.3%	(145)
Lots	20.1%	(288)	17.9%	(609)	30.4%	(437)	31.4%	(105)

There was a U-shaped relationship between degree of presence of intrinsic job characteristics and prevalence of smoking. Those who reported little or lots of intrinsic job characteristics were more likely to smoke than those who reported a moderate amount.

This relationship was particularly pronounced among the male non-manual workers and to a lesser extent among the male manual workers. Among the women there was a similar overall relationship

Table 11.11 Proportion who usually know the time at work classified by presence of intrinsic job characteristics

	Non-manual Male (n)	Female (n)	Manual Male (n)	Female (n)
Variety				
Little	59.5% (37)	67.0% (115)	61.9% (260)	63.8% (160)
Moderate	71.6% (102)	66.1% (254)	59.8% (306)	73.3% (135)
Lots	65.7% (271)	58.4% (579)	60.1% (649)	67.4% (178)
Responsibility				
Little	62.2% (37)	64.4% (149)	58.8% (204)	65.4% (159)
Moderate	70.9% (86)	64.0% (214)	60.4% (323)	74.6% (122)
Lots	65.9% (287)	59.8% (585)	60.8% (419)	65.4% (191)
Freedom to choose				
Little	63.4% (71)	68.3% (218)	53.0% (251)	68.7% (195)
Moderate	69.4% (98)	63.4% (273)	66.1% (301)	66.1% (112)
Lots	66.1% (239)	56.9% (452)	60.6% (655)	68.9% (164)
Promotion prospects				
Little	64.4% (104)	63.8% (398)	62.3% (681)	66.6% (353)
Moderate	70.5% (112)	61.3% (266)	57.8% (303)	75.0% (64)
Lots	65.2% (187)	58.5% (282)	56.8% (220)	68.8% (48)
Skill usage				
Little	65.3% (75)	69.9% (219)	57.3% (328)	66.0% (212)
Moderate	70.9% (86)	62.2% (238)	62.8% (290)	74.3% (101)
Lots	65.5% (249)	57.3% (489)	60.8% (587)	66.4% (152)
Recognition given				
Little	67.9% (106)	67.0% (233)	60.5% (506)	68.7% (198)
Moderate	69.1% (110)	58.8% (267)	60.4% (303)	71.3% (122)
Lots	64.8% (193)	60.3% (446)	59.8% (400)	67.3% (147)
Attention paid				
Little	62.6% (107)	66.9% (254)	58.8% (454)	67.1% (249)
Moderate	63.5% (115)	62.3% (292)	61.9% (339)	71.6% (102)
Lots	71.4% (185)	57.1% (399)	60.8% (406)	68.4% (114)
Overall				
Little	61.1% (18)	72.0% (75)	61.0% (287)	68.4% (196)
Moderate	71.3% (87)	64.8% (244)	62.0% (455)	69.0% (145)
Lots	65.5% (293)	58.3% (612)	58.7% (438)	70.1% (107)

among the non-manual workers but not among the manual workers. The U-shaped relationship was particularly apparent with certain of the intrinsic job characteristics. Those women who reported little and lots of skill usage, responsibility and recognition were more likely to smoke than those who reported a moderate amount of these characteristics. In addition, those female non-manual workers who reported little or lots of variety and attention were more likely to smoke than those who reported the presence of a moderate amount of these characteristics.

The various measures of time perception were considered as possible intermediary processes between the presence of these intrinsic job characteristics and smoking at work. As was the case with job structure, a comparable relationship with whether the workers usually knew the time at work was apparent.

Table 11.11 details the proportion of young adults who reported that they usually knew the time at work classified according to the degree of presence of the intrinsic job characteristics. An inverse U-shaped relationship was apparent. Those who reported little or lots of the intrinsic job characteristics were less likely to know the time than those who reported a moderate amount. Again this relationship was particularly pronounced among the male non-manual workers and to a lesser extent the female non-manual workers but it was apparent with six out of the seven intrinsic job characteristics among the female manual workers.

These findings would suggest that among these young adults those who report the presence of few intrinsic job characteristics work in a rather unstructured job situation. This lack of organization of their job routine provides the momentum for smoking. There was an atmosphere of timelessness. Sarah who used to work in a knitwear factory stiching little diamonds on jumpers all day epitomizes the tedium of this work routine (see Section 4.4). In this situation smoking could act as a marker of hours worked and hours to be worked.

Those who reported lots of intrinsic job characteristics were also less likely to know the time and more likely to smoke at work. This abundance of intrinsic job characteristics could be perceived as a form of stress by these young workers. Their greater involvement in their work seems to reduce their awareness of time. Smoking perhaps is a release from this immersion in their work - a means of reasserting their control over the flow of time. Some of the young workers reported in the interview that people smoked when they were under pressure (see Section 4.8). Smoking did not stop the pressure but it provided the smoker with a short respite from it.

It was noticeable that these relationships were less apparent among the male manual workers. It is possible that the degree of presence of other job characteristics is of greater importance to these young men than the "intrinsic" characteristic considered here.

11.8 Reasons for smoking at work

Table 11.12 details the reasons given by the young adults for smoking at work. As with their assessment of the reasons for smoking at home, the most popular reasons for smoking at work were "pleasurable relaxation" and "negative affect". However, compared with their assessments of reasons for smoking at home fewer of the smokers rated these, or any of the other reasons, as being of importance at work. In particular, the young people were less likely to rate "boredom" and "nothing to do" as reasons for smoking at work. This would agree with our previous finding that it was not "time dragging" but rather "not knowing the time" which was the more consistent intermediate variable between work situation and smoking. It would seem that at work smoking is less a means of passing the time and more a means of organizing the flow of time.

Table 11.12 Reasons for smoking at work

| | Non-manual | | Manual | |
	Male	Female	Male	Female
Stimulation	9.5%	10.5%	6.0%	7.9%
Manipulation	15.5%	16.0%	17.0%	21.1%
Relaxation	55.4%	58.6%	63.9%	67.9%
Negative affect	58.8%	71.9%	60.8%	79.4%
Addiction	47.6%	48.9%	59.5%	66.3%
Habit	42.4%	43.2%	50.9%	44.2%
"Boredom"	24.0%	27.1%	30.5%	26.5%
"Nothing to do"	40.4%	37.2%	54.2%	49.7%
Nmin	102	223	459	164

Table 11.12 also shows that at work smoking was perceived as a means of aiding relaxation. This would agree with our findings about the importance of breaks, and the role of smoking in creating breaks, as a means of creating personal space within a difficult work situation.

Smoking was also of importance as a means of coping with negative affect at work. This was particularly important among the women, as was the case with reasons for smoking at home. As in the case of Hilary (see Section 4.8), it seemed especially important to women as a means of controlling interpersonal conflict at work.

11.9 Summary

These findings confirm that the character of young people's working life is an important factor in explaining their smoking behaviour. The working conditions of the manual workers are especially conducive to smoking. Knowing the time emerged as an important intermediate variable between working conditions and smoking. In certain work situations the young people were less likely to know the time and more likely to smoke. Smoking seemed to be a useful means of controlling the passage of time in these situations. It enabled the workers to take breaks and to establish and reaffirm relationships with workmates. Other factors conditioned these relationships, in particular the smoking behaviour of workmates and the management policy on smoking at work.

12 The prevalence of smoking socially

12.1 Introduction

The interview study revealed that lesiure activity with their friends was the most valued aspect of the young people's day to day lives. It is also the setting in which smoking most frequently occurs. This chapter considers further the character of the young adults' leisure activities and the relationship of this to their smoking behaviour. While there is a wide variety of leisure activities only those mentioned in the interview study were considered. Since pub-life was frequently mentioned in the interviews special attention was given to this activity.

Table 12.1 Prevalence of smoking socially classified by perception of social time

		Male (n)	Female (n)
"Do you usually know what time it is?"	Yes	25.4% (673)	31.5%(988)
	No	32.5% (1657)	38.6%(1315)
"Do you usually care what time it is?"	Yes	29.3% (984)	33.8%(899)
	No	31.0% (1342)	36.8%(1403)
"Do you often feel that time drags?"	Yes	38.7%(212)	45.0%(191)
	No	29.7%(2087)	34.6%(2080)
"Do you often feel you waste your time?"	Yes	40.8%(397)	42.3%(503)
	No	28.1%(1908)	33.7%(1779)
"Are you often surprised at how quickly time has passed?"	Yes	30.6%(2156)	36.1%(2036)
	No	26.7%(180)	33.3%(267)

In the subsequent sections the relationship between the young adults' leisure activity and their smoking socially is summarized. Those who did not smoke when out socially in the evening were classified as non-smokers. In addition, bearing in mind Meissner's (1971) finding that the character of people's leisure activities is dependent upon the character of their work the main body of the analysis is confined to those with a job. This enables us to compare the importance of particular leisure activities for manual and non-manual workers. Again, the perception of time is considered as a possible intermediary variable. Table 12.1 details the prevalence of smoking when out socially classified by how time is perceived then. The young people who did not know the time and who thought that time dragged were significantly more likely to smoke when out socially.

12.2 Evening activities

The young adults indicated how frequently they participated in certain leisure activities each week. Table 12.2 details the prevalence of smoking socially classified according to the extent of the young people's involvement in these leisure activities. Of these three activities, the most popular was going to the pub, followed by playing sport and attending classes.

Table 12.2   Prevalence of smoking socially classified by involvement in leisure activities

	Non-manual Male (n)	Female (n)	Manual Male (n)	Female (n)
Go to pub				
Most evenings	49.1% (57)	44.6% (56)	50.0% (216)	54.2%(24)
Some evenings	24.4% (316)	24.1% (798)	36.4% (924)	34.5%(400)
Never	7.1% (42)	8.3% (108)	13.9% (101)	22.4%(49)
Play sport				
Most evenings	16.7% (18)	0% (15)	21.9% (73)	30.0%(10)
Some evenings	24.3% (255)	22.4% (483)	33.8% (648)	31.5%(162)
Never	30.9% (136)	25.7% (455)	42.9% (504)	35.2%(298)
Attend classes				
Most evenings	0% (3)	20.0% (5)	16.7% (6)	50.0%(2)
Some evenings	16.3% (86)	16.7% (245)	17.5% (143)	24.0%(75)
Never	29.1% (316)	26.1% (690)	39.4%(1059)	36.0%(392)

Participation in these activities was related to the sex and social class of the young adults. The men, especially those with manual jobs were more likely to go to the pub frequently. In addition, the men, especially those with non-manual jobs, were more likely to play sports frequently. The women with non-manual jobs were most likely to attend classes in the evening, followed by the men with non-manual jobs, the women with manual jobs and the men with manual jobs. Smoking was most prevalent among those who frequenly went to the pub in the evenings, irrespective of their sex and social class. It was least prevalent among those who frequently played sports or attended classes in the evenings.

Table 12.3 details the proportion of young people who usually knew the time when out socially classified according to the character of their leisure activities. The most consistent

144

relationship apparent is that those who played sport frequently were more likely to know the time. These are the people least likely to smoke when out socially. This would suggest that regular participation in sporting activities provides a clear structure to the young people's social lives such that the use of smoking as a means of imposing structure becomes of less value to them.

Table 12.3   **Proportion who usually know the time classified by involvement in leisure activities**

	Non-manual Male (n)	Female(n)	Manual Male(N)	Female(n)
Go to pub				
Most evenings	68.4%(57)	67.2%(58)	55.6%(216)	72.0%(25)
Some evenings	66.6%(314)	61.8%(795)	60.9%(925)	66.7%(399)
Never	58.5%(41)	61.0%(105)	64.7%(102)	74.0%(50)
Play sport				
Most evenings	10.0%(3)	10.0%(5)	66.7%(6)	50.0%(2)
Some evenings	69.3%(254)	62.8%(479)	60.9%(649)	72.0%(161)
Never	57.0%(135)	61.2%(456)	57.4%(507)	65.0%(300)
Attend classes				
Most evenings	10.0%(3)	10.0%(5)	66.7%(6)	50.0%(2)
Some evenings	69.0%(87)	57.6%(243)	56.3%(144)	68.0%(75)
Never	64.5%(313)	63.1%(689)	60.5%(1060)	67.2%(393)

Table 12.4 details the proportion of young adults who thought that time usually drags when out in the evenings. The most consistent relationship apparent is that those who attended classes frequently were least likely to think the time drags. These young adults were also less likely to smoke. This would suggest that attendance at night classes ensures that evenings are fully occupied. The use of smoking as a means of filling long unoccupied evenings would then be of less value to these young adults.

Table 12.4   **Proportion who think that time drags.**

	Non-manual Male(n)	Female(n)	Manual Male(n)	Female(n)
Go to pub				
Most evenings	37.5%(56)	51.7%(58)	64.3%(210)	68.0%(25)
Some evenings	37.5%(312)	49.2%(779)	59.1%(916)	68.8%(391)
Never	38.1%(42)	50.0%(104)	59.2%(103)	63.3%(49)
Play sport				
Most evenings	29.4%(17)	53.3%(15)	58.9%(73)	11.1%(9)
Some evenings	35.5%(251)	43.1%(473)	59.6%(644)	57.0%(158)
Never	43.4%(136)	55.7%(445)	60.7%(499)	75.6%(295)
Attend classes				
Most evenings	33.3%(3)	20.0%(5)	50.0%(6)	50.0%(2)
Some evenings	33.7%(86)	44.4%(241)	46.9%(143)	49.3%(73)
Never	38.5%(312)	51.4%(675)	62.1%(1049)	71.8%(386)

An additional reason why smoking is more prevalent among regular pub-goers and less prevalent among those who frequently play sports and attend classes maybe that the former occasion is more conducive to the sharing of cigarettes unlike the other two occasions. Table 12.5 considers this relationship. It shows that those smokers who played sport regularly were least likely to share cigarettes. The interview study suggested that the organized character of sporting activities leads to the development of strong social relations and so reduces the social value of smoking. This would agree with the lesser sharing of cigarettes by those who played sports. In addition, the unhealthy implications of smoking would ensure that it would be less accepted in a sporting context where the value of good physical health would be greater (see section 5.5).

Table 12.5 Proportion of smokers usually sharing cigarettes classified by involvement in leisure activities

	Non-manual		Manual	
	Male(n)	Female(n)	Male(n)	Female(n)
Go to pub				
Most evenings	59.3%(27)	52.0%(25)	56.2%(105)	69.2%(13)
Some evenings	61.1%(72)	57.9%(190)	54.8%(323)	57.4%(136)
Never	66.7%(3)	57.1%(7)	64.3%(14)	36.4%(11)
Play sport				
Most evenings	50.0%(2)	–	62.5%(16)	100% (3)
Some evenings	69.0%(58)	58.1%(105)	60.7%(211)	62.0%(50)
Never	48.8%(41)	56.0%(116)	49.8%(209)	54.4%(103)
Attend classes				
Most evenings	–	0%(1)	0%(1)	0%(1)
Some evenings	41.7%(12)	48.8%(41)	56.5%(23)	55.6%(18)
Never	62.5%(88)	59.1%(176)	55.9%(404)	57.6%(139)

The non-manual workers who attended evening classes were less likely to share cigarettes. This was not the case among the manual workers. This class difference possibly reflects a difference in the type of evening class attended. The non-manual worker possibly attends the more traditional evening class in which their is little opportunity for collaboration between students and, so, little opportunity for the sharing of cigarettes. Conversely, the manual workers possibly attends more workshop-type classes in which students collaborate on projects and in which the sharing of cigarettes is more valuable.

Finally, the women with manual jobs who frequently went to the pub were more likely to share cigarettes. This was not the case among the men. This probably reflects a sex and social class difference in the character of pub-going with it being more of a group experience for the manual female smokers.

Table 12.6 details the prevalence of smoking socially classified by the extent of the young people's alcohol consumption. There was an inverted U-shaped relationship between alcohol consumption and the prevalence of smoking. Those who drank little or a lot were less likely to smoke than those who drank a moderate amount or quite a lot. It was also noticeable that more women then men were complete abstainers whereas more men than women drank heavily.

Table 12.6   Prevalence of smoking socially classified by alcohol consumption

| | Non-manual | | Manual | |
	Male(n)	Female(n)	Male (n)	Female (n)
None	8.0%(25)	11.3%(97)	10.6%(66)	15.9%(63)
Little	18.5%(130)	17.7%(481)	27.3%(414)	33.3%(213)
Moderate	30.0%(217)	31.4%(347)	41.3%(601)	39.1%(174)
Quite a lot	41.0%(39)	48.8%(41)	55.8%(138)	53.3%(30)
A lot	25.0%(4)	40.0%(5)	60.6%(33)	-

A possible reason for this is shown in Table 12.7. This shows that those who drink a moderate amount or quite a lot were more likely to share cigarettes than those who drink little or none at all. This would suggest that the lighter drinkers tend not to be part of the 'pub-scene'. They have the occasional drink but do not participate in the social activity of the pub. Smoking and the exchange of cigarettes is of little value to them.

Table 12.7   Proportion of smokers usually sharing cigarettes classified by alcohol consumption

| | Non-manual | | Manual | |
	Male (n)	Female(n)	Male (n)	Female (n)
None	0%(2)	50.0%(10)	33.3%(6)	40.0%(10)
Little	56.5%(23)	57.1%(84)	52.8%(108)	50.7%(69)
Moderate	61.7%(60)	57.0%(107)	56.3%(240)	62.7%(67)
Quite a lot	68.8%(16)	60.0%(20)	58.7%(75)	68.8%(16)
A lot	100.0%(1)	50.0%(2)	60.0%(20)	-

The moderate drinker seems to be the one who enjoys the social life in pubs. Smoking and the exchange of cigarettes would be of particular value to them as a means of reaffirming their social relations there. This was the occasion when the 'crashing' of cigarettes was of particular importance (see section 5.2).

12.3   Companions

The young adults answered a series of questions about whom they socialized with in the evenings. Table 12.8 details the prevalence of smoking socially classified by their responses to these questions. This table shows that those who usually shared the evening with a group of friends were significantly more likely to smoke. An explanation for this is given in Table 12.9 which details the proportion of smokers who usually share their cigarettes when out socially. This shows that smokers are most likely to share their cigarettes when with a group of friends. Within the context of the group the exchange of cigarettes seems of particular importance as a means of maintaining the cohesivness of the group and of reaffirming the smokers status within the group (see section 5.2).

Table 12.8 Prevalence of smoking socially classified by details of social relations

	Non-manual Male(n)	Female(n)	Manual Male (n)	Female(n)
Usual companion				
Significant other	26.0%(223)	22.0%(667)	36.5%(830)	30.1%(349)
Close friend	25.7%(74)	29.9%(134)	37.6%(165)	53.8%(52)
Group of friends	35.7%(56)	29.7%(37)	52.0%(123)	62.5%(8)
Family	9.8%(41)	21.4%(103)	29.2%(96)	32.7%(55)
Alone	0 %(11)	35.3%(17)	28.6%(21)	50.0%(4)
Sex of companion				
Male	29.4%(68)	32.0%(25)	40.1%(147)	42.9%(14)
Female	40.0%(5)	21.3%(75)	47.4%(38)	36.6%(41)
Male and Female	25.6%(285)	24.4%(714)	36.1%(854)	37.1%(337)
Relationship between companions				
Close	25.9%(324)	25.0%(625)	37.9%(1071)	36.2%(354)
Other	26.7%(90)	20.6%(340)	32.9%(173)	29.8%(121)
Smoking Behaviour of friends				
Most smoke	14.7%(273)	12.3%(668)	19.8%(600)	19.0%(252)
Some smoke	42.2%(109)	46.6%(238)	49.7%(445)	46.9%(160)
None smoke	66.7%(33)	52.4%(63)	61.8%(204)	62.1%(66)

Most of the young people's friends were usually of both sexes. Among the small number whose companions were usually of the opposite sex smoking was most prevalent. The smokers were not especially more likely to share cigarettes if their companions were usually of the opposite sex (Table 12.9). Perhaps, smoking in this situation is useful as a means of controlling any difficulties in interpersonal relations (see section 12.5).

The majority of the young people reported that their friends were friends with each other indicating a close circle of friends. This was especially the case among the men with manual jobs. Those with such a close circle of friends were more likely to smoke. The smokers who had a close circle of friends were more likely to share cigarettes (Table 12.9). This would suggest that the social value of smoking increases as the degree of friendship between group members increases.

Finally, those whose friends smoked were more likely to smoke themselves (Table 12.8) and the smokers whose friends smoked were more likely to share their cigarettes (Table 12.9). These relationships confirm the importance of the group norm on the maintenance of smoking when out socially.

Table 12.9 Proportion of smokers usually sharing cigarettes classified by details of social relations

	Non-manual Male(n)	Female(n)	Manual Male(n)	Female(n)
Evening companions				
Significant others	60.0%(55)	56.2%(146)	51.4%(294)	53.4%(103)
Close friends	58.8%(17)	60.5%(38)	50.9%(57)	60.7%(28)
Group of friends	68.4%(19)	72.7%(11)	71.9%(64)	40.0%(5)
Family	50.0%(4)	38.1%(21)	73.1%(26)	66.7%(18)
Alone	-	83.3%(6)	50.0%(6)	10.0%(2)
Sex of companion				
Male	100.0%(2)	68.8%(16)	50.0%(18)	53.3%(15)
Female	57.9%(19)	62.5%(8)	59.3%(54)	60.0%(5)
Male and Female	64.7%(68)	54.7%(170)	58.0%(300)	60.2%(123)
Type of friendship				
Close	68.8%(80)	62.1%(153)	57.5%(391)	57.6%(125)
Other	31.8%(22)	46.4%(69)	42.9%(56)	52.8%(36)
Smoking behaviour of friends				
Most smoke	42.9%(35)	39.0%(82)	45.5%(112)	39.1%(46)
Some smoke	69.6%(46)	66.7%(108)	53.3%(214)	62.2%(74)
None smoke	71.4%(21)	68.8%(32)	69.4%(124)	68.3%(41)

12.5 Reasons for smoking socially

Table 12.10 details the proportion of the young smokers who agreed with the various reasons for smoking. As with homelife and worklife the most popular reasons for smoking socially were "relaxation" and "negative affect". The descriptions of the young people's leisure reveals that it is usually a shared experience with a group of friends. Within this context smoking and the sharing of cigarettes is important as a means of aiding relaxation with friends and of controlling negative affect.

Table 12.10 Reasons for smoking socially

	Non-manual Male	Female	Manual Male	Female
Stimulation	10.1%	6.4%	3.9%	7.2%
Manipulation	43.1%	29.6%	26.1%	32.1%
Relaxation	88.0%	80.8%	82.8%	85.1%
Negative affect	57.9%	80.9%	64.8%	84.5%
Addiction	46.8%	59.1%	65.4%	59.8%
Habit	59.4%	57.8%	58.7%	50.6%
"Boredom"	36.7%	37.3%	42.4%	46.2%
"Nothing to do"	40.7%	47.4%	57.1%	53.8%
Nmin	107	230	482	166

"Habit" and "addiction" were also identified as popular reasons for smoking. This would suggest that for many of the young adults leisure and smoking go together in the same way as work breaks and smoking go together. Indeed, smoking could be considered an extended break, a release from the responsibilities of home and work.

"Boredom" and "nothing to do" were less important reasons for smoking socially. Unlike homelife and worklife, what happened during leisure time was more likely to be something chosen to provide enjoyment and not something which would create boredom. Admittedly, those with a manual job were more likely to give 'boredom' and 'nothing to do' as reasons for smoking. These young people tended to spend less time in organized activities such as sports and evening classes. Time was more likely to drag for them, in their less structured social life. Consequently the value of smoking as a means of passing time was greater for them.

12.6 Summary

The survey findings reported in this chapter tend to confirm many of the inferences made in the comparable section of the interview study. It seems that for many of the young adults smoking during leisure serves a valuable social function. Particularly in unstructured social situations it acts as a means of reaffirming social relations and aiding relaxation. It also acts as a means of passing the time, although this function is of lesser importance.

13 Smoking and health-related behaviour

13.1 Introduction

In rational terms it would seem surprising that many people continue to smoke when there is so much evidence linking smoking with ill-health. However, evidence from our interview study (see chapter 7) suggested that many young adults consider smoking a minimal threat to their health since they defined health in a particular manner. This chapter considers further how young adults define health and how this is related to their smoking behaviour. In addition, it considers the character of other health-related behaviours and their relationship with smoking. It should be noted that the tests of significance used the chi-squared liklihood ratio statistics. In addition, although for ease of presentation, the tables present only details of sex differences, analyses considering differences between social classes were also performed and when they reached significance are referred to in the text.

13.2 Personal definition of health

In the interview study the young people gave a variety of definitions of health. The four most popluar definitions were: 1) the ability to carry on with usual activities, 2) fitness, 3) state of body, and 4) state of mind. To clarify the extent to which these definitions are related to the young people's smoking behaviour they were asked to indicate which of the four "best describes health". Table 13.1 details the proportion preferring each definition of health classified by their sex and smoking behaviour. The most popular definition was 'ability to carry on', followed by 'fitness', then 'state of body' and finally 'state of mind'. Among the young men there was a tendency for more of the light smokers and fewer of the heavy smokers to prefer the 'state of body' definition. Among the young women, those who smoked, especially the light smokers, were less likely to prefer the 'carry on' definition and were more likely than the non-smokers to prefer the 'fitness' and the 'state of mind' definitions. In general, more men than women preferred the 'fitness' definition whereas more women than men preferred the 'state of mind' definition. The latter difference reached significance. Further, the non-manual workers were consistently more likely to define health as a 'state of body' although this relationship did not reach significance.

Table 13.1 Personal definition of health

		(n)	Carry on with usual activities	Fitness	State of body	State of mind
Non-smoker						
	Male	(1091)	36.9%	29.7%	24.4%	9.0%
	Female	(1203)	39.3%	22.2%	25.5%	13.0%
Ex-smoker						
	Male	(306)	41.2%	26.1%	24.2%	8.5%
	Female	(374)	41.4%	22.7%	23.5%	12.3%
Light smoker						
	Male	(271)	36.9%	27.3%	28.4%	7.4%
	Female	(315)	30.5%	29.2%	23.5%	16.8%
Heavy smoker						
	Male	(604)	38.2%	30.6%	20.4%	10.8%
	Female	(405)	33.1%	26.2%	24.2%	16.4%

The definition of health preferred would thus seem to be related to both the sex, social class and smoking behaviour of the young adults. The young men's greater preference for 'fitness' as a definition reflects their greater concern about physical effectiveness (see section 13.4).

Among the young men, the lesser preference for 'state of body' as a definition by the heavy smokers would act as a protection against the content of traditional anti-smoking warnings. Conversely, the greater preference for this definition by the light smokers and by the non-manual workers, in general, suggests that their smaller consumption of cigarettes may be due to their greater susceptibility to such traditional warnings.

Among the young women, the greater preference for 'fitness' and the lesser preference for 'carry on' as definitions of health by the smokers may partly be a reflection of their perceptions of their own health status. As the following section shows, the women smokers have the poorest assessment of their own health status. However, most of them were probably able to perform their everyday activities thus invalidating 'carry-on' as a definition of health. However, many of them may have felt restricted in their performance of more strenuous activities thus emphasizing the 'fitness' definition of health. Finally, the greater preference for 'state of mind' as a definition of health among the female smokers may protect them against the content of the traditional anti-smoking warnings.

13.2 State of health

The young people were required to give an assessment on a four-point scale (excellent, good, fair, poor) of their health over the previous twelve months. They were also asked to answer 'Yes' or 'No' to a series of questions about their use of health services and any periods of illness they had during the previous six months. Tables 13.2 and 13.3 summarize their replies to these questions.

Table 13.2 Perceived health status

	(n)	Excellent	Good	Fair	Poor
Non-smoker					
Male	(1096)	37.8%	49.4%	11.8%	1.1%
Female	(1211)	25.0%	59.1%	14.4%	1.5%
Ex-smoker					
Male	(308)	26.6%	55.8%	15.9%	1.6%
Female	(375)	19.5%	56.3%	22.1%	2.1%
Light smoker					
Male	(271)	28.4%	54.6%	16.2%	0.7%
Female	(320)	16.9%	60.6%	19.1%	3.4%
Heavy smoker					
Male	(604)	20.7%	53.8%	21.9%	3.6%
Female	(451)	11.8%	55.2%	28.4%	4.7%

Table 13.2 shows that over half the young people classified their health as good and a further quarter classified it as excellent. Significantly more men than women and more non-smokers than smokers described their health as excellent. Among the smokers the heavy smokers were more likely than the light smokers to have a poor assessment of their health. Thus, in general, the smokers were less likely to define themselves as healthy.

Table 13.3 Six month health record

		Non-Smoker	Ex-Smoker	Light Smoker	Heavy Smoker
Visited doctor					
	Male	35.5%	44.7%	34.2%	41.4%
	Female	44.8%	55.4%	49.5%	56.1%
Confined to bed					
	Male	11.9%	16.3%	17.3%	14.1%
	Female	21.0%	19.9%	18.8%	22.9%
Taken medication	Male	39.4%	44.9%	41.9%	44.9%
	Female	46.0%	52.7%	50.8%	53.8%
Hospital out-patient					
	Male	21.6%	26.3%	23.6%	26.5%
	Female	19.1%	23.8%	23.9%	28.9%
Hospital in-patient					
	Male	4.5%	6.6%	4.4%	5.4%
	Female	7.9%	9.4%	6.9%	14.8%
Nmin	Male	1072	302	271	589
	Female	1172	363	303	439

Table 13.3 records the young people's health service usage. Overall, the heavy smokers had a significantly poorer health record. In the previous six months, the smokers were more likely than the non-smokers to have visited the doctor, been confined to bed, taken medication,been a hospital out-patient or been admitted to hospital. Overall, the women had a significantly poorer health record than the men. This accords with their self-definitions of their health status. Not only were smokers less likely than non-smokers to consider themselves healthy but they were also more likely to make use of the health service. There were no clear differences between the social classes.

13.4 Health practices and sporting activities

The converse of health education aimed at discouraging smoking and other unhealthy practices has been health promotion aimed at encouraging particular health practices and greater involvement in sporting activities. The young adults in this survey provided details of the extent to which they performed certain health practices and particular sporting activities. Tables 13.4 and 13.5 summarize their replies.

Table 13.4 Health practices

		Non-Smoker	Ex-Smoker	Light Smoker	Heavy Smoker
Weighs self regularly					
	Male	32.5%	36.6%	26.6%	26.9%
	Female	47.0%	48.1%	44.3%	43.3%
Uses margarine					
	Male	53.8%	62.3%	55.5%	57.6%
	Female	59.8%	65.4%	60.2%	60.1%
Drinks skimmed milk					
	Male	7.7%	10.5%	7.8%	8.8%
	Female	15.6%	15.5%	4.8%	14.6%
Brushes teeth daily					
	Male	91.7%	90.2%	91.1%	84.2%
	Female	98.5%	96.8%	97.2%	96.9%
Eats wholemeal bread					
	Male	31.5%	33.0%	41.1%	21.9%
	Female	48.7%	43.8%	50.3%	34.1%
Does not take sugar					
	Male	29.8%	30.4%	32.6%	21.6%
	Female	56.8%	59.5%	58.2%	50.2%
Nmin	Male	1089	305	270	603
	Female	1203	374	320	445

Table 13.4 shows that more women than men preferred each of the health practices whereas Table 13.5 shows that the men were more likely to run, cycle or do weight-training although the women were more likely to do keep-fit. Overall, the women were significantly more likely to perform the various health practices and less likely to participate in the sporting activities. This sex difference in their performance of these activities is

probably a reflection of a sex difference in attitudes to their bodies. Lerner and Karaberick (1974) reported that during late adolescence girls are more concerned about their bodies' physical attractivness whereas boys are more concerned about physical effectivness. In this survey the young women's greater performance of the various health practices and participation in keep-fit possibly reflects their greater concern about physical attractivnes. Similarly, the young men's greater involvement in running, cycling and weight-training would reflect a greater concern with physical effectivness. The performance of certain health practices and sporting activities was also related to the young people's smoking behaviour. The heavy smokers were least likely to weigh themselves regularly or to eat wholemeal bread but most likely to take sugar in their tea or coffee. They were also least likely to participate in any of the sporting activities. These heavy smokers would thus seem to be less concerned about their health, in general.

However, the light smokers differed less from the non-smokers in their performance of most of the health practices and sporting activities. Indeed, they were more likely than the non-smokers to eat wholemeal bread. Their participation in sporting activities may be a reason why these light smokers restrict their cigarette consumption because of their awareness that greater consumption would quickly impair their performance. This was the case with Sam in the army (see section 5.2).

Table 13.5 Sporting activities

		Non-Smoker	Ex-Smoker	Light Smoker	Heavy Smoker
Walks regularly					
	Male	51.6%	56.3%	51.5%	46.5%
	Female	54.2%	53.2%	55.4%	50.9%
Runs regularly					
	Male	35.4%	34.4%	27.4%	20.7%
	Female	10.0%	8.6%	13.7%	8.7%
Cycles regularly					
	Male	19.2%	15.9%	14.9%	9.7%
	Female	10.1%	7.4%	10.1%	5.5%
Does keep fit regularly					
	Male	45.3%	47.2%	43.0%	31.9%
	Female	47.7%	45.4%	47.7%	38.6%
Does weight training regularly					
	Male	25.9%	29.1%	23.5%	21.0%
	Female	5.2%	4.2%	5.4%	5.5%
Nmin	Male	1081	306	268	593
	Female	1202	372	320	448

The ex-smokers were more likely than others to weigh themselves regularly and to use margarine rather than butter. This possibly reflects a particular concern about any weight gain now that they have given up smoking.

Finally, the non-manual workers were more likely to perform the various health practices and to participate in the sporting activities. However, these relationships did not reach significance.

13.5 Respiratory health

An estimate of the effect of smoking on respiratory health was obtained from the young adults replies to a series of questions about respiratory symptoms. Table 13.6 summarizes their replies. This table shows a clear relationship between smoking and respiratory health. The smokers, especially the heavy smokers, were significantly more likely to report morning cough, morning phlegm, daytime phlegm, regular phlegm and shortness of breath. The men were more likely to report phlegm whereas the women were more likely to report shortness of breath.

Table 13.6 Respiratory symptoms

		Non-Smoker	Ex-Smoker	Light Smoker	Heavy Smoker
Morning cough	Male	5.7%	6.5%	13.4%	28.8%
	Female	4.8%	7.0%	10.1%	32.2%
Morning phlegm	Male	7.5%	10.4%	16.7%	32.3%
	Female	4.7%	6.4%	10.3%	23.7%
Daytime phlegm	Male	13.7%	18.6%	27.9%	41.5%
	Female	6.3%	7.2%	11.5%	28.3%
Regular phlegm (N=those with phlegm)	Male	11.7%(477)	13.0%(161)	21.1%(152)	32.1%(411)
	Female	8.3%(432)	12.4%(137)	8.0%(137)	26.8%(250)
Shortness of breath	Male	5.2%	6.1%	15.9%	25.7%
	Female	14.7%	21.9%	30.2%	49.4%
Nmin	Male	1046	295	258	591
	Female	1157	356	305	441

It is noticeable that on all these measures the ex-smokers also had more respiratory symptoms than did the non-smokers although not as much as did the smokers.

13.6 Beliefs about the health hazards of smoking

An assessment of the young adults' beliefs about the health hazards of smoking was obtained from their replies to the question which asked to what extent they agreed with three statements about smoking. Table 13.7 details the proportion who agreed with each statement classified by their sex and smoking behaviour.

Only a minority of the young adults agreed with any of the statements indicating a widespread awareness of the health hazards of smoking. This was particularly the case in their replies to the statement "Smoking is dangerous only to older people" indicating a special awareness of the vulnerability of young people. In addition, there was little difference between the smokers and non-smokers in their replies to this statement.

Table 13.7 Beliefs About Health Hazards of Smoking

		Non-Smoker	Ex-Smoker	Light Smoker	Heavy Smoker
Smoking is....					
only bad for you if	Male	20.9%	18.1%	23.4%	29.3%
you have been smoking	Female	15.6%	18.3%	18.0%	19.4%
for many years					
dangerous only to	Male	5.6%	4.0%	5.2%	8.0%
older people	Female	4.2%	5.2%	4.1%	3.8%
only bad for you if	Male	16.8%	16.8%	33.0%	32.3%
you smoke a lot	Female	12.5%	17.2%	26.9%	23.8%
Nmin	Male	1082	301	270	602
	Female	1200	370	316	449

However, the smokers were significantly more likely than the non-smokers to agree that "smoking is only bad for you if you smoke a lot" and the heavy smokers were significantly more likely than the others to agree that "smoking is only bad for you if you have been smoking for many years". Bearing in mind the previous table which showed the clear relationship between smoking and respiratory health this would suggest that the smokers are clearly underestimating the harmful effects of smoking. The women were significantly less likely to agree with the first and third statements indicating a greater awareness of the health hazards.

13.7 Summary

These results indicate that not only were the smokers, especially the heavy smokers, less likely to define themselves as healthy, but they were also more likely to report various signs and symptoms of ill-health and less likely to perform various health practices or sporting activities. Smoking, for the young people, would seem to be part of a larger unhealthy lifestyle.

The light smokers were less likely than the heavy smokers to define themselves as unhealthy and on many of the measures of health they were similar to the non-smokers. However, like the heavy smokers, they underestimated the health hazards of smoking. It is possible that in later years the cigarette consumption of these smokers would increase.

PART IV
CONCLUSIONS

14 A social model of smoking

14.1 Introduction

The aim of this book has been to increase our understanding of the process of smoking by young adults. It was noted at the outset that much previous research has tended to abstract smoking from its social context and to view it as a rather irrational behaviour pattern performed by individuals who have certain psychological inadequacies, e.g. susceptibility to peer pressure.

The approach adopted in our research was to view smoking as a meaningful experience to the smoker who lives within a certain social context. The aim of the book was to consider the different possible meanings of smoking within different contexts. This chapter summarizes our findings, places them within a broader societal framework and discusses the implications for attempts to discourage smoking.

It should be noted that the research did not aim to provide a comprehensive account of the social dynamics of smoking among young adults. Indeed, there are many inadequacies in the character of the data collected and of the analyses conducted. In particular, the interviews tried to obtain a broad picture of the young adults' lives in a relatively short time. It would have been useful to supplement the interviews with some participant observation-type research. Indeed, a few of the young people suggested such to us.

Further, in the reporting of data collected in interviews the researchers impose their framework on the findings. We have attempted to be aware of the various ideas which have influenced the way we have presented our findings. Researchers in the symbolic interactionist tradition have suggested that one way around this problem is to invite the study participants to comment on any interpretations of interviews. At the time of our interviews we suggested this to the young people and many of them were enthusiastic about the idea. However, as with the participant observation idea, time restricted us. Instead, we have quoted extensively from the interview transcripts to allow the young adults' views to come across clearly.

Concerning the survey findings, it should be emphasized that the results presented are part of a continuing project. It is intended to conduct more sophisticated statistical analyses of the data collected taking into consideration the careers of the young people during their adolescence.

Despite these criticisms, the text stands on it's own and it can at least be said that a start has been made.

14.2 Smoking in early adulthood

Early adulthood is a period when the young person is breaking away from the "adolescent life-structure" and forming a "preliminary adult identity" (Levinson, 1978). It is a period which "terminates the existing life structure and creates the possibility for a new one". It is a transitional period within which certain adult behavioural practices are established. Smoking can be considered one of these practices.

The survey results confirmed the findings of previous research in showing that smoking is a popular practice among many young adults. Considering the changing rate of increase in the prevalence of smoking from early adolescence to early adulthood it would seem that few people take up smoking after they reach their middle twenties. Many of the smokers expressed a desire to give up smoking and many had succeeded for varying lengths of time. However, most thought that it would be a difficult process although, again, many thought that they would actually succeed in either reducing their cigarette consumption or in stopping altogether. A large number had already given up but these seemed to be light smokers.

Many of the smokers reported an awareness of the health hazards of smoking but they continued to smoke. In an attempt to explain this apparent inconsistency our research considered the character of the immediate social context within which smoking occurred. The most popular occasion for smoking was during leisure time, followed by whilst at work and finally when at home. Within each of these contexts two important social psychological processes were apparent: the changing character of social relationships and the perception of time.

14.3 Social relations and smoking

It was apparent from both the interviews and the survey that the young adults' smoking behaviour occurred largely, but not completely, in the company of others. In this situation cigarettes were often exchanged. This was a useful means of establishing and reaffirming relationships with others.

In Goffman's (1967) terms, smoking was an important presentational ritual by which "the individual makes specific attestations to recipients concerning how he regards them and how he will treat them in the oncoming interaction". Through the exchange of of cigarettes "the recipient is told that he is not an island unto himself and that others are, or seek to be, involved with him and with his private concerns".

The work of Tajfel and his colleagues (e.g. Tajfel et al, 1971) into the social psychology of groups is of value in further understanding this process. Tajfel and Turner (1979) described a group as:

"a collection of individuals who perceive themselves to be members of the same social category, share some emotional involvement in this common definition of themselves and achieve some degree of social consensus about the evaluation of their group and their membership of it."

A central component of the formation and maintenance of the group is social categorization. This process induces individuals to define themselves in terms of their group membership. A series of experimental studies (see Turner, 1981) have shown that social categorization leads individuals to perceive themselves as similar to ingroup members and different from outgroup members. Smoking could be considered as part of this process of social categorization : by smoking certain individuals can clearly identify themselves as being members of a certain group and as not being part of another group. Eiser (1971) has also discussed this process with reference to smoking among adolescents.

At home, smoking was least common. In the parental home, where most of the young people still lived, relationships were sometimes strained. Indeed, many of the young people preferred to spend as little time as possible at home. In this situation, there was less of a sharing relationship with parents within which smoking could have a useful social function. Instead, smoking at home often occurred alone. In this situation, it was suggested that smoking was sometimes used as a substitute for companionship.

According to social categorization theory, smoking alone at home could be considered a means used by the smoker to differentiate himself from his family and to identify with friends, real or imagined, outside the home. Admittedly, not all the young adult smokers smoked alone at home. Some shared their cigarettes with other family members. These young people would be expected to identify more with their family. This would be especially the case with the young married couples where we noted a form of assortative mating. In this case, smoking together could be considered a means of defining themselves as a unit. Further, for some young mothers, sharing a cigarette with a friend could enable them to identify with the adult world and to disengage themselves, at least for a short period, from the world of their children (cf. Graham, 1978).

At work, smoking was more common. Many of the young adults stressed the importance of social relations at work. Especially in the manual workplace, the sharing of cigarettes helped to create a form of solidarity between the workers which enabled them to cope with the demands of the work.

In terms of social categorization theory, smoking could enable some of the workers to identify with their workmates or some of their workmates. Indeed, this aspect of smoking at work came across quite vividly in the interviews. Some workers on initial entry to their new place of work adopted smoking as a means of identifying with their new workmates. Others, did not identify with their workmates and so did not enter into a smoking relationship with them.

However, it was during leisure that smoking was most prevalent. The most popular venue for leisure was the pub. Here the young people met their friends and relaxed. Smoking and the exchange of cigarettes seemed to be an important aid to relaxation in this context.

Leisure occurred largely in groups. Again, the social categorization theory is a useful tool for explaining smoking within this context. Smoking could help in identification with one group and also help differentiate the smoker from another group. In our discussion of the image of the smoker (see Section 6.3) it was apparent that many young people identified smoking with a certain type of person. Consequently, observation of someone smoking would influence initial impression and subsequent social interaction with that person.

There was a social class difference in the character of the young adults' social life with manual workers being more involved in unstructured activities within which smoking was more valuable. It would seem that the over-controlled nature of their jobs encouraged these workers to prefer the more unstructured activities after work which would provide a release from the rules and restrictions of work (cf. Meissner, 1971).

14.4 Time and smoking

The study confirmed that for many of the young adults smoking was an important means of controlling the passage of time and in structuring time. It was a reminder of the importance of why an understanding of subjective time is crucial for explaining human action. This, of course, has been a central theme in the phenomenological literature . It is also an area that is attracting increasing interest within psychology and the social sciences in general. In reviewing research on the importance of subjective time in giving meaning to our lives Wessman and Gorman (1977) concluded:

"The time that we humans know is not just a cold, neutral objective sequence of happenings in the natural world. It is not something apart and detached, though we can intellectually conceive of it as such. Rather, the time that we experience and that most concerns us is our time, personal and social. It is related to the structure and the scope of our lives: the store of past memories, the worries and concerns, the future plans and aspirations. It is a vital personal time, fraught with continuity and significance, that we must grasp and shape in order to create the meaningful patterns of our lives".

At home, time dragged for many of the young adults. For them, smoking seemed a useful means of passing the time while waiting for possible excitement outside the home. In addition, some felt that they were wasting their time at home. They also were more likely to smoke, perhaps as a means of coping with the frustration of wasted time.

The way the young people perceive time at home can be considered within the context of the stage of their development. According to Erikson (1963) this is the period when people develop the capacity for intimacy. This is the period when young people are preparing for long-term relationships and marriage. These activities would generally take place outside the parental home where some of the young people would feel increasingly restricted. For them especially time would pass slowly and they would feel they were wasting vital opportunities.

At work many of the young people often felt that they did not know the time, it was unstructured. For them smoking, and the breaks which smoking provided, was a useful means of structuring the day. Smoking was a means of marking out the passage of time.

The character of subjective time at work was related to the characteristics of the young adults' work. Many were disappointed at the lack of excitement and opportunity in their work. In this atmosphere of low demand nothing seemed to change for the young worker. Alternatively, some young workers experienced high demand at work. There was little opportunity to separate themselves from their work and to orient themselves with reference to objective time.

At leisure some of the young people felt that time dragged . To these young people smoking could help impose some structure on the flow of time and also to pass the time. Again this was particularly relevant to the young manual workers who especially participated in unstructured activities.

These are the young people whose lives Corrigan (1978) vividly described. Their immediate environment offers them little excitement. Instead, they often hang about the streets waiting for something to happen. As one young man in Corrigan's book noted they often spend their evenings "just about in the streets deciding what to do with the time".

14.5 Health and smoking

Health and illness are not fixed entities but rather they are created and sustained through an interaction of social, psychological and biological factors. The interviews and survey revealed that the young adults defined health and illness in a variety of ways and that these definitions were related to their sex, social class and smoking behaviour. So, too, was their performance of various health and sporting practices.

The young men more frequently preferred an activity definition of health and participated in more strenuous sporting activities. The young women more often preferred a psychological definition of health and performed various health practices more frequently but various sporting activities more rarely than did the men. It was suggested that this reflected sex differences in the way the young people defined themselves. The non-manual workers preferred a more physiological definition of health and performed more health practices and participated in more sports than did the manual workers.

Within these frameworks, the health hazards of smoking would be perceived differently by men and women and by manual and non-manual workers. Among the men smoking would not be perceived as a threat unless it impaired physical performance. Among the women it would be less likely to be perceived as a threat unless it impaired their psychological health and ability to carry on. The manual workers, more of whom smoke, would underestimate the health hazards of smoking because of their lesser concern about the 'state of their body' and their lesser participation in organised sporting activities.

14.6 Societal context of smoking

In designing our research we criticized the traditional psychological approach adopted by many previous investigators of smoking behaviour. Instead, we preferred a more social psychological approach which concentrated on the character of young people's social interaction and on how they viewed smoking within the context of their own lives. However, in drawing conclusions we cannot ignore the wider societal context within which the young people live and within which smoking occurs. Indeed, as Corrigan (1978):

"in so far as we construct our problems apart from society then our conclusions are located outside the political process of change in that society".

We have emphasized that smoking has certain valuable meanings to many young adults but this does not mean that it is inevitable that they continue to smoke. Rather, smoking is of value to them because of their location in society and also because of the ability of the tobacco monopolies to create and reinforce an image of smoking as socially acceptable and personally beneficial.

The young adults live in a society which condemns many of them to dead-end jobs, to unemployment and to social isolation. It is a society in which the tobacco industry exerts tremendous influence on the government to ensure that they have maximum opportunity to promote sales of their products. It is within this wider societal framework that smoking remains a valuable activity for many young adults. If the effectivenes of anti-smoking campaigns is to be increased they must develop their strategy with an awareness of this societal framework.

This is a criticism that has attracted much support within health education. A recent report from the World Health Organisation summarized the need for the discipline to reject the traditional "victim-blaming" approach:

"In the past health care providers have focussed mainly on the modification of individual behaviour, implying that the individual is responsible for his plight. This approach blames the sick, the poor, and the miserable for their illness, their poverty and their misery. It ignores the fact that in a number of situations it is not the individual who needs to be charged but the social environment in which he or she lives. In other words, the political, economic and environmental factors that have a negative or neutralising effect on healthy behaviour need to be modified".

In the final section some suggestions are made in this respect regarding attempts to discourage smoking among young adults.

14.7 Deterring smoking

Our research has shown that smoking is rooted in the social relations experienced by young people. It follows that efforts to deter smoking must consider how to arrange social relations so as to reduce the value of smoking. Discussing a similar implication in the development of social work practice Corrigan and Leonard (1978) referred to Marx's third thesis on Feuerbach, viz.

"The materialist doctrine that men are products of circumstances and upbringing, and that, therefore, changed men are the products of other circumstances and changed upbringing, forgets that it is men that change circumstances and that the educator himself needs educating".

By placing smoking both within its immediate social context and within the wider societal context we reveal the magnitude of the task facing the health educator. The implications of this are that health educators must reassess their role in improving the health of society. Previously (Murray and Jarrett, 1985a,b) we have made some suggestions about the need to develop a more materialist and socially and personally relevant health education. Such an education would need to consider the basis of the different forms of social relations as well as relating it's message to the everyday concerns of young people. In addition, the form of any health education must be based upon an understanding of how young people define health. Here we develop this theme further.

Considering homelife, it is accepted (Duck, 1986) that family relationships are much more intense and emotionally charged than other relationships. Economic hardship can bring emotional turmoil into the home. For example, some of the interviews illustrated how unemployment can bring conflict into family relations. Smoking is an important means used by some young people to cope with such conflict. Attempts to reduce smoking in the home must consider the economic realities of family life. At the most basic level, there must be sufficient resources available to ensure that the whole family can lead a decent life.

At home the young person also smoked as a means of identifying with the family or with friends outside the family. In addition, he smoked to pass the time or because he was frustrated at time being wasted at home. However, these factors were conditioned by their parents' attitude to smoking and their parents' own smoking practices. During adolescence the young person develops an attitude towards smoking which is related to that of their parents (Murray et al, 1985). For this reason, anti-smoking

167

education needs to be directed not only at young people but also at their parents. The recent development of school-based anti-smoking campaigns which involve the parents is an important development in this respect (Reid, 1985).

Work was often a soul-destroying experience for many of the young adults. The survey showed that both low demands and high demands on the young worker encouraged smoking. Attempts to discourage smoking must consider the need to re-organise working relationships. In discussing this previously (Murray and Jarrett, 1985b) we referred to a U.S. Department of Health, Education and Welfare report entitled **Work in America** published in 1973. That report concluded:

> "What workers want most, as more than 100 studies in the past 20 years show, is to become masters of their immediate environment and to feel that their work and they themselves are important".

The research conducted in the subsequent fifteen years has in no way reduced the relevance of that conclusion.

Entry to work was often an unsettling experience for many of the young people. There seemed to be little guidance given to prepare them for the world of work. Instead they had to learn quickly how to adapt to the ways of older workers in order to survive. Dorn (1984) has suggested that a means of making school health education more relevant to young people is to integrate it into general careers education and preparation for adult life. By combining anti-smoking education with such careers guidance the health educator is not only easing the young person's transition into working life but also increasing the relevance of the health message.

Among the unemployed, smoking was especially important as a means of passing the time. For these young people the days seemed endless. Jahoda (1982) has documented the deleterious effects on mental health of long-term unemployment. It is obviously essential that urgent steps need to be taken to increase employment opportunities and to provide comprehensive educational and leisure facilites for these young people. In addition, unemployment benefit needs to be raised to a level which enables the young person to participate more fully in social life.

In this era of high unemployment health educators need to be aware of the special needs of the unemployed. Their anti-smoking message must relate to the particular experiences of these young people. Its effectiveness could be increased if it was integrated into an advice service for young people to provide them with assistance on how to cope with the pressures of unemployment.

The prevalence of smoking was high among the housewives. These women face a variety of particular problems. Alone with their children for a large proportion of the day many of these women experience social isolation and emotional and physical exhaustion. Gove (1972), among others, has pointed to the higher levels of mental illness among these women. There is obviously a need for substantial improvement in childcare facilities such that women have the opportunity of entering into the labour market. Haavio-Mannila (1986) has shown, with reference to historical and cross-cultural evidence, that the greater the involvement of women in the workforce the lower the prevalence of mental illness among them.

There is a need for the development of day-time facilities for housewives and their children such that the women can have the opportunity of participating in various activities other than childcare and housework. Further, as Graham (1984) has clearly demonstrated, lack of support places intolerable demands on many working class women. "New policies to meet the health needs of families in the 1980's require recognition that the present system of distribution allocate fewest resources to those who have most responsibility".

Finally, preparation for motherhood, needs to be an important priority within health education. Indeed, a wider preparation for parenthood could alert young men as to their responsibilities in the home. Within this context, it would be possible to develop anti-smoking education that was related to the actual experience of family life.

For many young people smoking is an integral part of their social life. Indeed, for many it epitomizes relaxation and enjoyment. The sharing of cigarettes identifies the smoker as an adult and as part of the group. The popularity of smoking was related to the character of the young people's leisure activities. It was especially prevalent in the pub which was the most popular venue for social activities. There is a need to develop a wider range of leisure facilities for young people. However, since the character of young people's leisure is related to the character of their work attempts to reorganize leisure would be difficult unless it was linked to changes in working practices such as those previously described.

Health education must pay particular attention to the character of the social scene within which smoking occurs. Dorn's (1984) suggestion regarding the integration of school health education into education for adult life is useful. Such a technique would increase the relevance to the anti-smoking message to young people about to leave school.

Overall, of course, steps must be taken to curb the power of the tobacco monopolies to promote their wares. This would involve the implementation of a wide range of restrictive measures such as those proposed by the Royal College of Physicians (1983). As it stated:

> "Curtailment of smoking must be an essential part of the policy of any government sincerely concerned with the health of the people it serves".

In addition, such a government would need to address the social and societal context of smoking if it is to be successful in eradicating this modern epidemic.

Appendix

OUTLINE OF QUESTIONNAIRE

SECTION I: GENERAL DETAILS

1. What sex are you?

2. What is your marital status?

3. How many children do you have?

4. How old were you when you left school?

5. Who do you live with?

6. Do you own a car?

7. Do you own a motorbike?

8. What is your work status?

SECTION II: WORK

A. Those with full time jobs

1a. What job do you actually do?

1b. Did you need particular qualification/training?

2a. To what extent are the following features present in your work?
    a. Variety
    b. Responsibility
    c. Being able to choose your own method of working
    d. Chance of promotion
    e. Chance to use your abilities
    f. Recognition for good work
    g. Attention paid to suggestions
    h. Stress
    i. Boredom

3a. Do you usually work alone?
b. Are most of your workmates the same sex as yourself?
c. Do you work shifts?
d. Are you paid piece-rate?
e. Are you required to clock-on?
f. Do you work overtime regularly?
g. Was this the job you wanted to do when you left school?
h. Would you say you get on well with the people who have been at your workplace a lot longer than you?
i. Do you have 'official' breaks which allow you to stop working for short periods of time?(apart from mealbreaks)
j. Do you take breaks other than official breaks?
k. Is there a special place for you to go to during breaktimes. i.e. are you able to leave your job?
l. Do you usually spend your breaks talking to workmates?
m. Is it possible to buy cigarettes at your place of work?

4. Is smoking allowed in your workplace?

5. Do people you work with smoke?

6. Do your workmates offer their cigarettes around?

B. **Those without a full time job outside the home**

1. How long is it since you held a full time job?

2. How oftern do you do the following
   a. Housework
   b. Shopping
   c. Childcare
   d. Visit friends or family
   e. Nothing special
   f. Other

3. Who do you usually spend your time with during the day?

4. Do you plan your day in advance?

SECTION III   LEISURE

1. How often do you do the following in the evening?
   a. Watch TV
   b. Go to the pub
   c. Play sport e.g. Football/Swimming
   d. Play games e.g. Pool/Darts
   e. Attend classes
   f. Housework
   g. Nothing special
   h. Other

2. How often do you do any of the following?
   a. Go for a walk (other than going about your usual activities)
   b. Go for a run or a jog
   c. Cycle
   d. Do Keep-Fit exercises
   e. Weight training

172

3. Who do you usually spend your evenings with?

4. Are your friends male or female?

5. How many of your workmates do you see socially?

6. Would you say that most of your present friends are people you grew up with?

7. Would you say that most of your close friends are also friends with each other?

8. When in the pub do you play darts or pool or other pub games?

9. How much alcohol do you usually drink each week?
   Glasses of wine, Pints Lager/Beer, Pints of Cider, Single measures of spirits?

10. How much alcohol do you drink?

11. How many of the friends you usually spend time with outside work smoke?

12. If your friends smoke do they usually offer their cigarettes around?

SECTION IV: SMOKING

1. Have you ever smoked? (If you answered No, go to question 19)

2. Do you smoke now?
   a. Daily
   b. Occasionally
   c. Not at all
   (If you answered not at all go to question 18, otherwise continue to answer the following questions)

3. What do you you usually smoke?
   Manufactured cigarettes, Hand-rolled cigarettes, Pipe, Cigars?

4. What brand of cigarettes/cigars do you usually smoke or what kind of tobacco? Please give brand name and tar level.

5. a. If you smoke cigarettes, how many do you smoke a day on weekdays?
      How many cigarettes a day to you usually smoke at weekends?

   b. If you smoke a pipe or roll your own cigarettes, how many ounces or grams of tobacco do you usually smoke each week?

   c. If you smoke cigars, how many cigars a week to do you usually smoke?

6. Please indicate how many cigarettes you smoke or whether you smoke a pipe or cigars in the following situations.
   a. At work or at home during the day
   b. At home in the evening
   c. Out socially in the evening

7. How often do you share your cigarettes with the following?
   a. Family
   b. Workmates
   c. Friends

8. How often do you smoke alone in the following situations?
   a. At home
   b. At work
   c. Socially

9. Do you inhale tobacco smoke?

10. How old were you when you started to smoke regularly?

11. a. Have you ever tried to give up smoking altogether?
11. b. How many times have you given up smoking for a week or more?

12. Would you like to give up smoking?
    (If you answered Yes, what is the main reason?)
    a. Cost
    b. Concern for your health
    c. Pregnancy
    d. Doctor's advice
    e. Something you read or saw on TV
    f. Pressure from friends or family
    g. Other

13. Do you think you would feel healthier if you gave up smoking?

14. Are you concerned about putting on weight if you gave up smoking?

15. How difficult do you think it would be for you to give up smoking?

16. Do you ever limit your smoking because of pressure from family or friends?

17. Please show whether you agree or disagree with the following. Please answer for each situation, at work, at home and socially
    a. I smoke to keep myself from slowing down
    b. Handling and lighting up a cigarette is part of the enjoyment of smoking it
    c. Smoking is pleasant and relaxing
    d. When I feel uncomfortable, upset or angry about something, I smoke
    e. I smoke when I am bored
    f. I really want to smoke if I haven't done so for a while
    g. I smoke automatically without being aware of it
    h. I smoke when I have nothing to do

18. **For Ex-Smokers Only**
    a. How often did you smoke?
       Daily/Occasionally/Only once or twice
    b. How long is it since you gave up smoking?
    c. What was it like for you to give up smoking?
    d. What was the main reason for you giving up?
       Cost
       Concern for you health
       Doctor's advice
       Pregnancy
       Something you read or saw on TV
       Pressure from friends or family
       Other

19. What do you think you will be doing in 10 years time?
    a. Smoking 20 cigarettes or more a day
    b. Smoking less than 20 cigarettes a day
    c. Smoking cigarettes only occasionally
    d. Smoking a pipe or cigars
    e. Not smoking at all

20. Please describe the smoking habits of each person listed
    below
    a. Wife/husband
       Boyfriend/girlfriend
    b. Mother
    c. Father

21. How many people of your age smoke?

22. Please indicate how much you agree with the following
    a Smoking is only bad for you if you have been smoking for
       many years
    b. Smoking is dangerous only to older people
    c. Smoking is only bad for you if you smoke a lot

SECTION V: TIME

1. Please answer the following for when you are at work, at
   home, and out socially. Please answer for each situation
    a. Doyou usually know what time it is withoutlookingat
       your watch?
    b. Do you usually care what time it is?
    c. Do you often feel that time drags by?
    d. Do you feel you often waste your time?
    e. Are you often surprised at how quickly time has passed?

SECTION VI: HEALTH

1. People think of health in different ways. Which of the
   following do you think best describes health?
    a. Ability to carry on with usual activities
    b. Fitness
    c. State of body
    d. State of mind

175

2. How would you describe your health over the past 12 months?
   a. Excellent
   b. Good
   c. Fair
   d. Poor

3. Do you ever do things to keep healthy?

4. During the last six months have you done any of the following?
   a. Visited your doctor for anything other than contraceptive reasons.
   b. Been so ill you have had to stay in bed
   c. Taken any medication
   d. Been to hospital out-patients for any reason, e.g. x-ray, ante-natal care
   e. Been admitted to hospital

5. Do the following apply to you?
   a. Usually weigh self at least once a week?
   b. Usually use margarine instead of butter?
   c. Usually drink skimmed milk?
   d. Usually brush teeth daily?
   e. Usually eat wholemeal bread?
   f. Usually take sugar in tea or coffee?

6. Do you usually cough first thing in the morning in winter?

7. Do you usually bring up any phlegm from your chest first thing in the morning in winter?

8. Do you bring up any phlegm from your chest during the day in winter?

9. If you answered Yes to question 7 or 8, do you bring up phlegm like this for as much as three months each year?

10. Do you get short of breath when hurrying on flat ground or walking up a slight hill?

References

Action on Smoking and Health, Northern Ireland (1986). **The Economic Consequences of Smoking in Northern Ireland.** Belfast: Ulster Cancer Foundation.

Ajzen, I., Fishbein, M. (1980) **Understanding Attitudes and Predicting Social Behaviour** New Jersey: Prentice Hall.

Banks, M.H., Bewley, B.R., Bland, J.M., Dean, J.R., Pollard,V. (1978). Long-term study of smoking by secondary schoolchildren. **Archives of Disease in Childhood** 53: 12 - 19.

Baric, L. (1979). **Primary Socialisation and Smoking.** London: Health Education Council.

Bewley, B.R., Bland, J.M. (1978). The child's image of a young smoker. **Health Education Journal** 37: 236 - 241.

Bewley, B.R., Johnson, M.R.D., Banks, M.H. (1979). Teacher's smoking. **Journal of Epidemiology and Community Health** 33: 219 - 222.

Blaxter, M., Paterson, E. (1983). **Mothers and Daughters.** London : Heinemann.

Brehm, J.W. (1966). **A Theory of Psychological Reactance.** New York : Academic Press.

Clarke, J., Hall, S. Jefferson, T., Roberts, B. (1976). Subcultures, cultures and class: a theoretical overview. In S. Hall, T. Jefferson (eds.) **Resistance Through Rituals.** London: Hutchinson.

Corrigan, P. (1978). **Schooling the Smash Street Kids.** London: MacMillan.

Corrigan, P., Leonard, P. (1978). **Social Work Practice under Capitalism : A Marxist Approach.** London : MacMillan.

Day, S. (1982). Is obstetric technology depressing? **Radical Science Journal** 12: 17 - 42.

Department of Health, Education and Welfare (1973). **Work in America** Cambridge, Mass.: M.I.T. Press.

Dobbs, J., Marsh, A. (1983). **Smoking among Secondary Schoolchildren.** London, H.M.S.O.

Doll, R., Hill, A.B. (1952). A study of the aetiology of carcinoma of the lung. **British Medical Journal 2:** 1271 - 1276.

Dorn, N. (1984). **Alcohol, Youth and the State.** Beckenham: Croom Helm.

Duck, S. (1985) **Human Relationships: An Introduction to Social Psychology.** London: Sage.

Eiser, J.R. (1981). Smoking and health : what can social psychology contribute? **International Journal of Mental Health 9** : 164 - 181.

Erikson, E.H. (1963). **Childhood and Society.** New York : Norton.

French Committee for Health Education and Sofres Communication (1983). Young people and smoking. **European Monographs in Health Education Research 4:** 9 - 75.

Goffman, E. (1967). **Interaction Ritual: Essays on Face-to-Face Behaviour.** New York: Doudleday.

Gove, W.R. (1972) Sex roles, marital roles and mental illness. **Social Forces 51:** 34 -44.

Graham, H. (1976). Smoking in pregnancy; the attitudes of expectant mothers. **Social Science and Medicine 10:** 398 - 405.

Graham, H. (1984). **Women, Health and the Family.** Brighton: Wheatsheaf.

Griffin, C. (1985). **Typical Girls? Young Women from School to the Job Market.** London: Routledge and Kegan Paul.

Haavio-Mannila, E. (1986). Inequalities in health and gender. **Social Science and Medicine 22:** 141 - 149.

Harre, R., Secord, P.F. (1972). **The Explanation of Social Behaviour.** Oxford : Blackwell.

Hollis, M. (1977). **Models of Man.** Cambridge: Cambridge University Press.

Jacobson, B. (1986). **The Ladykillers.** London : Pluto

Jahoda, M. (1982). **Employment and Unemployment : A Social Psychological Analysis.** Cambridge : Cambridge University Press.

Lee, P.N. (1976). **Statistics of Smoking in the United Kingdon.** London : Tobacco Research Council.

Lerner, R.M., Karabenick, S.A. (1974). Physical attractivness, body attitudes and self-concept in late adolescents. **Journal of Youth and Adolescence 3:** 307 - 310.

Levinson, D. J. (1978). **The Seasons of a Man's Life.** New York: Alfred A. Knopf.

McKennell, A.C., Thomas, R.K. (1967). **Adults' and Adolescents' Smoking Habits and Attitudes.** London : H.M.S.O.

McQueen, D. (1985). Behavioural research in smoking : new opportunities. **Quarterly Journal of Social Affairs 1:** 283 - 291.

Marklund, U. (1979). **Smoking in Compulsory Schools.** Goteborg: Institute of Education, University of Goteborg.

Marsh, A., Matheson, J. (1983). **Smoking Attitudes and Behaviour** London : H.M.S.O.

Marsh, P., Rosser, E., Harre, R. (1978). **The Rules of Disorder** London : Routledge and Kegan Paul.

Meissner, M. (1971). Long arm of the job : A study of work and leisure. **Industrial Relations 10:** 239 - 260.

Morgan, M., Eiser, J.R., Budd, R.J., Gammage, P., Gray, E. (1986). Patterns of cigarette smoking among Bristol schoolchildren. **Health Education Research 1:** 95 - 100.

Morris, J.N. (1979). Social inequalities undiminished. **Lancet 1:** 95 - 100.

Murray, M. (1983). The social context of smoking during adolescence. In W. Forbes, R. Frecker, D. Nostbakken (eds) **Proceedings of the 5th World Conference on Smoking and Health** Ottowa : Canadian Council on Smoking and Health.

Murray, M., Cracknell, A. (1980). Adolescents' views on smoking. **Journal of Psychosomatic Research 24:** 243 - 251.

Murray, M., Jarrett, L. (1985a). Young people's perception of health, illness and smoking. **Health Education Journal 44:** 18 - 22.

Murray, M., Jarett, L. (1985b). Young people's perception of smoking at work. **Health Education Journal 44:** 22 - 26.

Murray, M., Kiryluk, S., Swan, A.V. (1984). School characteristics and adolescent smoking. **Journal of Epidemiology and Community Health 38:** 167 - 172.

Murray, M., Kiryluk, S., Swan, A.V. (1985). Relation between parents' and children's smoking behaviour and attitudes. **Journal of Epidemiology and Community Health 39:** 169 - 174.

Murray, M., Swan, A.V., Bewley, B.R., Johnson, M.R.D. (1983). The development of smoking during adolescence - the MRC/ Derbyshire Smoking Study. **International Journal of Epidemiology 12:** 185 - 192.

Murray, M., Swan, A. V., Johnson, M. R. D., Bewley, B. R. (1983). Some factors associated with increased risk of smoking by children. **Journal of Child Psychology and Psychiatry 24:** 223 - 232.

Murray, M., Swan, A.V., Enock, G. (1981). **A Study to Evaluate the Effectiveness of a Health Education Programme ('My Body') on Primary Schoolchildren. Report of the Second Stage of the Evaluation.** London, Submitted to Health Education Council.

Murray, M., Swan, A.V., Mattar, N. (1983). The task of nursing and risk of smoking. **Journal of Advanced Nursing 8:** 131 - 138.

O.P.C.S. (1985). **General Household Survey 1984.** London : H.M.S.O.

Reid, D. (1985). Prevention of smoking among schoolchildren: recommendations for policy development. **Health Education Journal 44:** 3 - 12.

Royal College of Physicians (1983). **Health or Smoking?** London: Pitman.

Tajfel, H., Flament, C., Billig, M.G., Bundy, R.F. (1971). Social categorization and intergroup behaviour. **European Journal of Social Psychology 1:** 149 - 177.

Tajfel, H., Turner, J.C. (1979). An integrative theory of intergroup conflict. In W.G. Austin, S. Worchel (eds) **The Social Psychology of Intergroup Relations.** Monterey, California: Brooks/Cole.

Tomkins, S. (1966). Psychological model for smoking behaviour. **American Journal of Public Health 56:** 17 - 20.

Turner, J.C. (1981). The experimental social psychology of intergroup behaviour. In J.C. Turner, H. Giles (eds) **Intergroup Behaviour.** Oxford: Blackwell.

Warr, P., Cook, J., Wall, T. (1979). Scales for the measurement of some work attitudes and aspects of psychological well-being. **Journal of Occupational Psychology 52:** 129 - 148

Wessman, A.E., Gorman, B.S. (1977). The emergence of human awareness and concepts of time. In A.E. Wessman, B.S. Gorman (eds) **The Personal Experience of Time.** New York: Plenum.

Willis, P. (1977) **Learning to Labour.** Aldershot: Gower.

World Health Organisation (1983). **New Approaches to Health Education in Primary Health Care.** (WHO Technical Series No. 690). Geneva: WHO.

Index

Index